4-9-51

BOOKS FOR TIRED EYES

AMERICAN LIBRARY ASSOCIATION ·

LIST OF BOOKS IN LARGE PRINT

FOURTH EDITION

BOOKS

FOR TIRED EYES

A LIST OF BOOKS IN LARGE PRINT

Compiled by CHARLOTTE MATSON *and* LOLA LARSON
Minneapolis Public Library

Chicago

AMERICAN LIBRARY ASSOCIATION

1951

Preface

ALL THE BOOKS on this list are printed in type at least as large as that of the list (12-point), and they are all well spaced and clearly printed. Books marked * are in type as large or as legible as 14-point, and ** indicates 18-point. The list for children includes no book in type smaller than 14-point, and ** indicates 18-point or larger type. On the adult list † indicates a book that has been found to be of interest to the 14-, 15- and 16-year-old group and to young adults. In the second part, books are either grouped by ages for which they are suited, or individually graded. The grade designation follows the price.

Such a list as this cannot include all the excellent books printed in large type, nor does it pretend to be a list of only the best titles, but it does represent a variety of interesting, readable books, set in good clear type and chosen with due regard for the differing tastes of readers. Since it is meant to be a reading rather than a buying list, a few books no longer in print have been included because of their content or because of their exceptionally good print. Most of these will be found in the collections of the larger libraries.

The compilers hope that this list will be of value to many readers.

C. M.
L. M. L.

Contents

Contents (continued)

Contents (continued)

Adult Books

Treasure Hunts

Armstrong, Charlotte. Unsuspected. Coward. $2.50

† Balmer, Edwin, and Wylie, Philip. After Worlds Collide. Lippincott $2.75

† ———— When Worlds Collide. Lippincott. $2.75

Barbeau, Marius. Mountain Cloud. Caxton. $4

*† Buchan, John. Prester John. Houghton. $3

Canning, Victor. Golden Salamander. M. S. Mill. $3

Collins, Norman. Black Ivory. Duell. $2.50

† Conrad, Joseph. Lord Jim. Doubleday. $2.50

———— Nigger of the Narcissus. Doubleday. $2

———— Nostromo. Doubleday. $2

———— Typhoon. Doubleday. $2.50

* Coolidge, Dane. Yaqui Drums. Dutton. $2.50

Evans, Allen Roy. Reindeer Trek. Coward. $2.50

† Friend, Oscar J. The Kid from Mars. Fell. $2.50

*† Gail, Otto Willi. By Rocket to the Moon. Dodd. $2.50

Gallico, Paul. Adventures of Hiram Holliday. Knopf. $2.50

Greene, Graham. Heart of the Matter. Viking. $3

———— Ministry of Fear. Viking. $2.50

Hammond-Innes, Ralph. Gale Warning. Harper. $2.50

† Hewes, Agnes D. Jackhammer: Drill Runners of the Mountain Highways. Knopf. $2.50

Hubbard, L. Ron. Slaves of Sleep. Shasta. $3

Iams, Jack. Prematurely Gay. Morrow. $2.75

Kauffmann, Stanley. The Hidden Hero. Rinehart. $3

† Kipling, Rudyard. Captains Courageous. Doubleday. $2.75

1

*† Leinster, Murray. The Last Space Ship. Fell. $2.50

  Miller, Warren H. Tiger Bridge. Page. $2

  Morgan, Bryan S. Vain Citadels. Little. $2.75

† Nordhoff, Charles, and Hall, James N. Hurricane. Little. $2.75

† Skidmore, Hubert. River Rising! Doubleday. $2.25

  Teilhet, Darwin L. Something Wonderful to Happen. Appleton.
      $2.75

  Vance, Ethel. Escape. Little. $2

  Walker, David. The Storm and the Silence. Houghton. $2.75

Man's Best Friend

† Atkinson, Eleanor. Greyfriars Bobby. Harper. $2.50

† Chamberlain, George A. Overcoat Meeting. A. S. Barnes. $2.50

† ———— Scudda-hoo, Scudda-hay. Grosset. $1

† Chipperfield, Joseph E. Storm of Dancerwood. Longmans. $3

  Davis, Richard H. Bar Sinister. Scribner. $2

*† Hinkle, Thomas C. Barry. Morrow. $2

*† ———— Bing. Morrow. $2

*† ———— Buckskin. Morrow. $2

*† ———— Cinchfoot. Morrow. $2

*† ———— King. Morrow. $2

† Holt, Stephen. Phantom Roan. Longmans. $2.50

† James, Will. The Dark Horse. Grosset. $1.49

† ———— Smoky. Scribner. $2.50

† London, Jack. White Fang. Grosset. $1

† Meek, Sterner S. Dignity, Springer Spaniel. Knopf. $2.50

† Meyers, Barlow. Last of the Wild Stallions. Westminster. $2.50

* Morley, Christopher. Where the Blue Begins. Lippincott. $2.50

  Nathan, Robert. Journey of Tapiola. Knopf. $1.75

*† O'Brien, Jack S. Silver Chief to the Rescue. Winston. $2.50

*† ———— Valiant, Dog of the Timberline. Winston. $2.50

† O'Hara, Mary. My Friend Flicka. Lippincott. $2.75

  Orwell, George. Animal Farm. Harcourt. $1.75

  Patton, Don. The Bunch Quitter. Caxton. $3

† Rawlings, Marjorie K. The Yearling. Scribner. $3
† Rosman, Alice G. Jock the Scot. Putnam. $2
  Salten, Felix. Forest World. Bobbs. $2.50
  ——— Perri. Bobbs. $2.50
  ——— Renni. Bobbs. $2.50
  Starr, John C. Black Dinah. Caxton. $3.50
† Terhune, Albert P. Further Adventures of Lad. Grosset. $1
*† ——— Lad: A Dog. Dutton. $2.75
** ——— Real Tales of Real Dogs. Saalfield. $1

Hearth and Home

† Aldrich, Bess S. White Bird Flying. Appleton. $2.50
  Bach, Marcus. The Dream Gate. Bobbs. $3
  Beresford-Howe, Constance. Unreasoning Heart. Dodd. $2.50
  Bonavia-Hunt, Dorothy A. Pemberley Shades. Dutton. $3
  Brown, Joe D. Stars in My Crown. Morrow. $2.75
  Buck, Pearl. East Wind, West Wind. World Pub. $1
  Campbell, Grace. Higher Hill. Duell. $2.75
† ——— Thorn-Apple Tree. Duell. $2.50
  Carfrae, Elizabeth. Portrait of Caroline. Putnam. $2.75
† Carroll, Gladys H. As the Earth Turns. Macmillan. $1.98
† Cather, Willa S. My Antonia. Houghton. $3
† ——— O Pioneers! Houghton. $3
  Charles, Joan. Son and Stranger. Harper. $2.50
† Chase, Mary Ellen. Windswept. Macmillan. $3
  Chase, Virginia. American House. Duell. $2.75.
  Colver, Alice R. Kingsridge. Macrae. $2.50
  Compton-Burnett, Ivy. Bullivant and the Lambs. Knopf. $3
  Deasy, Mary. The Hour of Spring. Little. $3
  Erdman, Loula G. Lonely Passage. Dodd. $2.75
† Ferber, Edna. Show Boat. Grosset. $1.49
  Fleury, Barbara F. Faith the Root. Dutton. $2.75
  Gipson, Alice E. Silence. Caxton. $2.50
* Howard, Warren. Such Happy People. Arcadia. $2

3

Innis, Mary Q. Stand on a Rainbow. Duell. $2.50
* Kantor, MacKinlay. The Good Family. Coward. $2
Kavanagh, Patrick. Tarry Flynn. Devin-Adair. $2.75
* Kehoe, Karon. City in the Sun. Dodd. $2.50
Kent, Louise A. Mrs. Appleyard's Year. Houghton. $2
Kirkbride, Ronald. Spring Is Not Gentle. Doubleday. $3
† Lane, Rose W. Let the Hurricane Roar. Longmans. $1.75
Laverty, Maura. Touched by the Thorn. Longmans. $2.50
Lyon, Marguerite. Take to the Hills. Grosset. $1
McCrone, Guy. Aunt Bel. Farrar. $3
Martin, George V. Our Vines Have Tender Grapes. Grosset. $1
Mitford, Nancy. Love in a Cold Climate. Random. $2.75
Molloy, Robert. Uneasy Spring. Macmillan. $2.75
Mori, Toshio. Yokohama, California. Caxton. $3
* Moser, Edwa. Roundelay. Duell. $2.75
Neville, Lee. Poplars Across the Moon. Page. $2
Ogilvie, Elisabeth. Rowan Head. McGraw. $3
Pakington, Humphrey. Young William Washbourne. Norton. $3
† Rice, Alice H. Mrs. Wiggs of the Cabbage Patch. Appleton. $2.50
* Richter, Conrad. Always Young and Fair. Knopf. $2
† Runbeck, Margaret L. Pink Magic. Houghton. $2.75
Shaw, Lau. The Quest for Love of Lao Lee. Reynal. $3
Sohn, Monte. The Flesh and Mary Duncan. Dodd. $2.75
Stevenson, Dorothy E. Young Mrs. Savage. Rinehart. $2.75
† Tarkington, Booth. Alice Adams. Grosset. $1.49
Thorpe, Berenice. Reunion on Strawberry Hill. Knopf. $2.50
Thorseth, Matthea. Cradled in Thunder. Superior Pub. $3
Tomkinson, Grace. Welcome Wilderness. Washburn. $2.50
Undset, Sigrid. Images in a Mirror. Knopf. $2
Whipple, Dorothy. The Priory. Macmillan. $2.50
† Wiggin, Kate D. Mother Carey's Chickens. Houghton. $2.50

Past Glories

Adams, Samuel H. Banner by the Wayside. Random. $3

Aldrich, Bess S. Lieutenant's Lady. Grosset. $1.49

Allis, Marguerite. Water Over the Dam. Putnam. $3

Andrews, Mary R. S. Perfect Tribute. Scribner. $1.25

Atkinson, Eleanor. Johnny Appleseed. Harper. $2

Beach, Rex. World in His Arms. Putnam. $2

Binns, Archie. Land Is Bright. Scribner. $3

Boyd, James. Bitter Creek. Scribner. $3

† ———— Drums. Scribner. $2.50

† Bristow, Gwen. Handsome Road. Grosset. $1.49

Brooks, Anne T. Smoke on the River. Arcadia. $2

† Cannon, LeGrand, Jr. Look to the Mountain. Holt. $2.75

**† Cather, Willa S. Death Comes for the Archbishop. Knopf. $2.75

† Coatsworth, Elisabeth. Toast to the King. Coward. $2

*† Crane, Stephen. Red Badge of Courage. Heritage. $3.50

Davis, Harold L. Beulah Land. Morrow. $3

† Dickens, Charles. Tale of Two Cities. Dodd. $2.75

Edmonds, Walter. The Wedding Journey. Little. $2.50

Fast, Howard. American. Duell. $1

———— Citizen Tom Paine. Duell. $2.75

———— Patrick Henry and the Frigate's Keel. Duell. $2.50

† Ferber, Edna. Cimarron. Grosset. $1.49

Forbes, Esther. Johnny Tremain. Houghton. $3

Forester, Cecil S. African Queen. Modern Library. $1.25

———— Beat to Quarters. Little. $2

———— Captain from Connecticut. Little. $3

———— Commodore Hornblower. Little. $2

———— Lord Hornblower. Little. $2.50

———— Ship of the Line. Little. $2

Frost, Elizabeth H. Mary and the Spinners. Coward. $2.50

Gann, Ernest K. Benjamin Lawless. Sloane. $3.50

Gruber, Frank. Broken Lance. Rinehart. $2.50

Guthrie, Alfred B. The Way West. Sloane. $3.50

Hamon, Marcel. Nightfall at Noon. Ziff-Davis. $2.50

Hart, Scott. Eight April Days. Coward. $2.50

† Hawes, Charles B. Dark Frigate. Little. $2.50

† ——— Charles B. Mutineers. Little. $2.25

Hergesheimer, Joseph. Bright Shawl. Knopf. $2.50

Heyer, Georgette. Reluctant Widow. Putnam. $3

† Hubbard, Margaret A. Flight of the Swan. Bruce. $3

Ibn-Sahav, Ari L. Jessica, My Daughter. Crown. $3

† Janvier, Thomas A. Aztec Treasure House (for Boys). Macmillan.
$3

Kelleam, Joseph E. Blackjack. Sloane. $3

Kossak, Zofia. The Meek Shall Inherit. Roy. $3

Lagerkvist, Pär. The Dwarf. Fischer. $2.50

McCall, Marie. Evening Wolves. Day. $3

Mann, Thomas. Beloved Returns: Lotte in Weimar. Knopf. $2.50

——— Joseph and His Brothers. Knopf. $2.75

——— Joseph in Egypt. Knopf. $2.75

——— Joseph the Provider. Knopf. $3.50

——— Young Joseph. Knopf. $2.75

Marshall, Effie L. Ruth. Falmouth Pub. $2.50

Murphy, Edward F. Scarlet Lily. Grosset. $1

† Nordhoff, Charles, and Hall, James N. Falcons of France. Little.
$2.75

Payne, Robert. The Yellow Robe: A Novel of the Life of Buddha.
Dodd. $3

Pinckney, Josephine. Great Mischief. Viking. $2.75

Putnam, George P. Hickory Shirt, a Novel of Death Valley in 1850.
Duell. $2.75

Remarque, Erich M. All Quiet on the Western Front. Little. $2.75

Richter, Conrad. The Fields. Knopf. $2.50

——— The Trees. Knopf. $2.75

Rooney, Philip. Golden Coast. Duell. $2.50

† Scott, Walter. Talisman. McKay. $2.50

† Stevenson, Robert Louis. Black Arrow. Scribner. $3

Stone, Irving. The Passionate Journey. Doubleday. $3

Tarbell, Ida M. He Knew Lincoln. Macmillan. $1.75

Terrot, Charles. The Passionate Pilgrim. Harper. $2.75

Thane, Elswyth. The Queen's Folly. Duell. $2.50

Van de Water, Frederic F. Catch a Falling Star. Duell. $3

† Wheelwright, Jere H., Jr. The Strong Room. Scribner. $3

Wilder, Thornton. The Ides of March. Harper. $2.75

† Wilson, William E. Abe Lincoln of Pigeon Creek. McGraw. $3

Fair Warning

Blake, Nicholas. Head of a Traveler. Harper. $2.50

Bonnamy, Francis. Blood and Thirsty. Duell. $2.50

Brady, Leo. Edge of Doom. Dutton. $3

Brean, Herbert. The Darker the Night. Morrow. $2.50

———— Wilders Walk Away. Morrow. $2.50

Brown, Zenith J. False to Any Man. Scribner. $2

Canning, Victor. Chasm. Mill-Morrow. $3

Chandler, Raymond. Farewell, My Lovely. Knopf. $2

———— The Little Sister. Houghton. $2.50

† Chesterton, Gilbert K. Father Brown Omnibus. Dodd. $3

Cheyney, Peter. Dark Wanton. Dodd. $2.50

Christie, Agatha. The Hollow. Dodd. $2.50

Clark, Philip. The Dark River. Simon. $2

Cohen, Octavus R. Danger in Paradise. Macmillan. $2

Coxe, George H. Inland Passage. Knopf. $2.50

———— Lady Killer. Knopf. $2.50

Crane, Frances. Indigo Necklace. Grosset. $1

Dean, Amber. Snipe Hunt. Crime Club. $2.25

Debrett, Hal. Before I Wake. Dodd. $2.50

Disney, Dorothy C. Hangman's Tree. Random. $2.50

Dodge, David. The Long Escape. Random. $2.50

† Doyle, Arthur Conan. Boys' Sherlock Holmes. Harper. $2

Eberhart, Mignon. House of Storm. Random. $2.50

———— Wolf in Man's Clothing. Grosset. $1

Fearing, Kenneth. The Big Clock. Harcourt. $2.50

Fox, James. Death Commits Bigamy. Coward. $2.50

Frost, Barbara. The Corpse Said No. Coward. $2.50

Gallagher, Gale. Chord in Crimson. Coward. $2.50

Gardner, Curtiss T. Bones Don't Lie. Mill. $2

Gardner, Erle S. Case of the Cautious Coquette. Morrow. $2.50

———— Case of the Lazy Lover. Grosset. $1

———— Clue of the Runaway Blonde; and, Clue of the Hungry Horse. Grosset. $1

———— D. A. Takes a Chance. Morrow. $2.50

Goldman, Raymond L. Death Plays Solitaire. Coward. $2

Goldthwaite, Eaton K. Root of Evil. Duell. $2.50

Gruber, Frank. The Leather Duke. Rinehart. $2.50

Heberden, Mary V. Engaged to Murder. Crime Club. $2.25

Iams, Jack. Do Not Murder before Christmas. Morrow. $2.50

Kane, Frank. Green Light for Death. Washburn. $2.50

King, Rufus. Case of the Redoubled Cross. Doubleday. $2.25

Knight, Clifford. Hangman's Choice. Dutton. $2.50

Knight, Kathleen M. Bass Derby Murder. Doubleday. $2.25

Lee, Thorne. Monster of Lazy Hook. Duell. $2.50

Leslie, Joan. Shoes for My Love. Doubleday. $2

Lobaugh, Elma K. I Am Afraid. Doubleday. $2.25

Long, Manning. Savage Breast. Duell. $2.50

Nelson, Hugh L. Ring the Bell at Zero. Rinehart. $2.50

Piper, Evelyn. The Innocent. Simon. $2.50

Quale, Anthony. On Such a Night. Little. $2

Reilly, Helen. Staircase 4. Random. $2.50

Revell, Louise. Bus Station Murders. Macmillan. $2

Rinehart, Mary R. Haunted Lady. Rinehart. $2

Scherf, Margaret. Gun in Daniel Webster's Bust. Doubleday. $2.25

Sherry, Edna. No Questions Asked. Dodd. $2.50

Simenon, Georges. Blind Alley. Harcourt. $2.50

Stein, Aaron Marc. Drop Dead. Doubleday. $2

Stout, Rex. Second Confession. Viking. $2.50

———— The Silent Speaker. Viking. $2.50

Thayer, Lee. Evil Root. Dodd. $2.50

* Treat, Lawrence. F as in Flight. Morrow. $2.50

———— T as in Trapped. Morrow. $2.50

* Van Dine, S. S. Winter Murder Case. Scribner. $1.75

Watkins, Alex. Shadow for a Lady. Mill. $2.50

Waugh, Hillary. The Odds Run Out. Coward. $2.50

Gay Enchantment

Adams, Samuel H. Perfect Specimen. Liveright. $2

Bangert, Ethel E. Delta Girl. Arcadia. $2

Berridge, Elizabeth. It Won't Be Flowers. Simon. $2.75

Burt, Katharine N. Strong Citadel. Scribner. $3

* Carter, Anne. The Enchanted Year. Arcadia. $2

Chase, Mary E. Mary Peters. Macmillan. $1.98

* Cunningham, Louis A. Evergreen Cottage. Arcadia. $2

* Dean, Terry. Key to Happiness. Arcadia. $2

De Leeuw, Cateau. The Gentle Heart. Macrae. $2.50

* Denniston, Elinore. Girl from Nowhere. Dodd. $2.50

† DuMaurier, Daphne. Rebecca. Doubleday. $3

Garrison, Joan. Dear Cathy. Arcadia. $2

Hall, Bennie C. Both Were Young. Arcadia. $2

Hancock, Lucy A. Doctor Bill. Macrae. $2.50

Hill, Grace L. Amorelle. Grosset. $1

———— April Gold. Grosset. $1

———— Beauty for Ashes. Grosset. $1

———— Beloved Stranger. Grosset. $1

———— Challengers. Grosset. $1

———— Chance of a Lifetime. Grosset. $1

———— Daphne Deane. Grosset. $1

* ———— Duskin. Grosset. $1

* ———— Found Treasure. Grosset. $1

———— Gold Shoe. Grosset. $1

———— Head of the House. Grosset. $1

———— Marigold. Grosset. $1

———— Matched Pearls. Grosset. $1

* Hill, Grace L. Partners. Grosset. $1
———— Patricia. Grosset. $1
———— Ransom. Grosset. $1
* ———— Red Signal. Grosset. $1
* ———— The Search. Grosset. $1
———— Silver Wings. Grosset. $1
* ———— Stranger Within the Gates. Grosset. $1
———— Substitute Guest. Grosset. $1
———— Voice in the Wilderness. Grosset. $1
———— Where Two Ways Meet. Grosset. $1
Ilyin, Boris. Green Boundary. Houghton. $3
Larrimore, Lida. Each Shining Hour. Macrae. $2
Loring, Emilie. Fair Tomorrow. Grosset. $1
———— Swift Water. Grosset. $1
* Lynd, Leslie. The Tender Melody. Arcadia. $2
Milne, Alan A. Two People. Dutton. $2.50
Nathan, Robert. Winter in April. Knopf. $2
* Parmenter, Christine W. Big Book of Parmenter Romances. Grosset.
$1.49
† Porter, Gene S. Freckles. Grosset. $1.49
Prouty, Olive H. Lisa Vale. Houghton. $2.50
———— Stella Dallas. Houghton. $2.50
Renault, Mary. Return to Night. Morrow. $3
Walker, Dorothy P. Five O'Clock Surgeon. Macrae. $2.50

Old Favorites

† Austen, Jane. Pride and Prejudice. Heritage. $3.75
————. ———— Macrae. $2.50
————. ———— World Pub. $1.25
† ———— Sense and Sensibility. Dodd. $2.75
* Balzac, Honoré de. Old Goriot. Heritage. $3.75
† Barrie, James M. Sentimental Tommy. Scribner. $3.50
Bennett, Arnold. The Old Wives' Tale. Heritage. $5
*† Borrow, George. Lavengro (Ed. for Young People). Houghton. $2

* Carroll, Lewis. Alice in Wonderland. Heritage. $2.75
* ———— Through the Looking Glass. Heritage. $2.75
  Cooper, James Fenimore. Deerslayer. Scribner. $2.50
† ———— Last of the Mohicans. Scribner. $2.50
  ———— Pilot. Minton, Balch. $1.75
† DeFoe, Daniel. Robinson Crusoe. McKay. $2.50
  Dickens, Charles. Bleak House. Heritage. $3
  ———— Christmas Carol. Garden City. $1.98
† ———— David Copperfield. Dodd. $2.75
  ———— Great Expectations. Dodd. $2.50
  ———— Mystery of Edwin Drood. Heritage. $3
  ————Oliver Twist. Dodd. $2.75
† Dumas, Alexandre. Count of Monte Cristo. Heritage. $5
  Goldsmith, Oliver. Vicar of Wakefield. Heritage. $3.75
*† Hale, Edward E. Man Without a Country. Random. $1
* Hardy, Thomas. Under the Greenwood Tree. Macmillan. $3.50
† Hudson, William H. Green Mansions. Knopf. $6
* James, Henry. The Turn of the Screw. Heritage. $3.50
† Kingsley, Charles. Westward Ho! Heritage. $5
*† Loti, Pierre. Iceland Fisherman. Knopf. $3
* Melville, Herman. Moby Dick. Heritage. **$5**
† Porter, Jane. Scottish Chiefs. Scribner. **$3**
* Prévost d'Exiles. Antoine François, Abbé. *Story of Manon Lescaut and the Chevalier des Grieux.* Heritage. **$5**
  Sterne, Lawrence. . . . Tristram Shandy. Heritage. $5
† Stevenson, Robert L. Black Arrow. Scribner. $3
† ———— Kidnapped. Scribner. $3
† ———— Treasure Island. Scribner. $2.50
† Stowe, Harriet B. Uncle Tom's Cabin. Coward. $2.50
*† Swift, Jonathan. Gulliver's Travels. Heritage. $3.75
† Verne, Jules. Mysterious Island. Scribner. $3
† ———— Twenty Thousand Leagues Under the Sea. World Pub. $1.25
  ————. ———— Scribner. $2.50
* Zola, Emile. Nana. Heritage. $5

Short Story Harvest

Allen, Hervey. It Was Like This. Rinehart. $1.50

Aswell, Mary L., ed. The World Within. McGraw. $3.75

Benét, Stephen V. Tales before Midnight. Rinehart. $2.50

Bleiler, Everett F., and Dikty, T. E., eds. Best Science Fiction Stories, 1949. Fell. $2.95

Bond, Nelson. The Thirty-first of February (Fantastic Stories). Gnome Press. $3

Bond, Raymond T., ed. Famous Stories of Code and Cipher. Rinehart. $3.50

Burnett, Whit, and Burnett, Hallie, eds. Story: The Fiction of the Forties. Dutton. $3.95

* Butler, Ellis P. Pigs Is Pigs. Doubleday. $1

Capote, Truman. A Tree of Night and Other Stories. Random. $2.75

Connolly, Cyril, ed. Horizon Stories. Vanguard. $2.75

Conrad, Joseph. Youth. Doubleday. $2.50

Demetrios, George. When Greek Meets Greek. Houghton. $2.75

† Donovan, Frank P., Jr., and Henry, Robert S., eds. Headlights and Markers (Railroad Stories). Creative Age. $2.75

Enright, Elizabeth. Borrowed Summer and Other Stories. Rinehart. $2.50

Eustis, Helen. The Captains and the King Depart. Harper. $2.75

Fast, Howard. Departure and Other Stories. Little. $3

Foley, Martha, ed. Best American Short Stories. Houghton. 1946 $3. 1947 $3.50

† Hart, Bret. Luck of Roaring Camp. Macmillan. $1.32
——— Tales of the Gold Rush. Heritage. $3.75

† Haycraft, Howard, ed. Boys' Second Book of Great Detective Stories. Harper. $2.75

Hudson, William H. Tales of the Gauchos. Knopf. $3

Jessup, Alexander, ed. Representative Modern Short Stories. Macmillan. $5

† Kipling, Rudyard. Complete Stalky and Co. Doubleday. $3

LaFarge, Christopher. All Sorts and Kinds. Coward. $3

Lincoln, Victoria. Grandmother and the Comet. Rinehart. $2.50

*† Macauley, Thurston. Great Horse Omnibus. Ziff-Davis. $5

MacMahon, Bryan. The Lion-Tamer and Other Stories. Dutton. $2.75

McNulty, John. Third Avenue, New York. Little. $2

Maxwell, James A. I Never Saw an Arab Like Him. Houghton. $2.50

Milne, Alan A. Birthday Party. Dutton. $3

Nathan, Robert. They Went On Together. Knopf. $2

O'Hara, John. Pipe Night. Duell. $2.50

Olcott, Frances J., comp. Good Stories for Anniversaries. Houghton. $3

Pirandello, Luigi. The Medals and Other Stories. Dutton. $2.75

Porter, Katherine A. Pale Horse, Pale Rider: Three Short Novels. Harcourt. $2.50

Rawlings, Marjorie K. When the Whippoorwill. Scribner. $3

Richter, Conrad. Early Americana. Knopf. $2.50

Runyon, Damon. In Our Town. Wilcox & Follett. $1

Saroyan, William. My Name Is Aram. Harcourt. $2.50

† Self, Margaret C. Treasury of Horse Stories. A. S. Barnes. $3.75

Strode, Josephine. Social Insight Through Short Stories. Harper. $3

Thomason, John W. Marines and Others. Scribner. $3

Wechsberg, Joseph. Sweet and Sour. Houghton. $2.75

Weiskopf, Franz C., ed. Hundred Towers: An Anthology of Creative Czechoslovak Writing. Wyn. $3.50

Spurs and Saddles

Brand, Max. Mountain Riders. Grosset. $1

———— Silvertip's Chase. Grosset. $1

———— Silvertip's Search. Grosset. $1

Clay, Weston. Bar-M Boss. Phoenix. $2

Coolidge, Dane. Wally Laughs-Easy. Dutton. $2.50

Drago, Harry S. Lost Buckaroo. Dodd. $2

* ———— Rustlers' Bend. Doubleday. $2.50

Ernenwein, Leslie. Rebels Ride Proudly. Dutton. $2.50
Evans, Evan. Gunman's Legacy. Harper. $2.50
Field, Peter. End of the Trail. Grosset. $1
————— Outlaw Valley. Jefferson House. $2.50
————— Powder Valley Showdown. Grosset. $1
Floren, Lee. Milk River Range. Phoenix. $2
Fox, Norman A. Shadow on the Range. Dodd. $2
Grey, Zane. Arizona Ames. Grosset. $1
————— Border Legion. Grosset. $1
————— Fighting Caravans. Grosset. $1
————— Forlorn River. Grosset. $1
————— Knights of the Range. Grosset. $1
————— Lost Wagon Trail. Grosset. $1
————— Nevada. Grosset. $1
————— Rainbow Trail. Grosset. $1
————— Shepherd of Guadaloupe. Grosset. $1
————— Stairs of Sand. Grosset. $1
————— Sunset Pass. Grosset. $1
————— Thunder Mountain. Grosset. $1
————— Trail Drivers. Grosset. $1
————— West of the Pecos. Grosset. $1
————— Wild Horse Mesa. Grosset. $1
* Gruber, Frank. Broken Lance. Rinehart. $2.50
————— Smoky Road. Rinehart. $2.50
Halleran, Eugene E. Outlaw Trail. Macrae. $2.50
* ————— Rustlers' Canyon. Macrae. $2.50
Haycox, Ernest. Long Storm. Grosset. $1
* Heckelmann, Charles N. Guns of Arizona. Doubleday. $2.50
Holmes, Llewellyn P. Desert Rails. Simon. $2
Hopkins, Tom J. The Hard Riders. Doubleday. $2.50
Hopson, William L. New Cowhand. Phoenix. $2
* ————— Outlaw of Hidden Valley. Phoenix. $2
James, Will. In the Saddle with Uncle Bill. Scribner. $2.50
* Kelliher, Dan. Western Cowboy. Phoenix. $2

14

* Manning, Roy. Two Gun Sheriff. Macrae. $2.50
O'Rourke, Frank. Thunder on the Buckhorn. Random. $2.50
Raine, William M. Bandit Trail. Houghton. $2.50
Rister, Claude. Points West. Phoenix. $2
Robertson, Frank C. Longhorns of Hate. Dutton. $2.50
*† Santee, Ross. The Bubbling Spring. Scribner. $3.75
† Schaefer, Jack. Shane. Houghton. $2.50
Short, Luke. Fiddlefoot. Riverside Press. $2.50
——— Ramrod. Macmillan. $2
Shott, Abel, pseud. Brothers of the Brand. Phoenix. $2
——— Solo Saddles. Phoenix. $2
Strong, Charles S. Buckskin Pards. Phoenix. $2
——— North of Santa Fe. Phoenix. $2
——— Red River Crossing. Phoenix. $2
Tompkins, Walker A. Manhunt West. Macrae. $2.50
Westland, Lynn. Man from Montana. Phoenix. $2

Novels from Life

* Angell, Richard. The Long Swim. Putnam. $2.25
Atkinson, Oriana. Big Eyes. Appleton. $3
Baker, Dorothy. Our Gifted Son. Houghton. $2.75
Baker, Sherman. Bradford Masters. Dutton. $2.75
† Bell, Margaret E. The Totem Casts a Shadow. Morrow. $2.50
* Bolton, Isabel. The Christmas Tree. Scribner. $2.75
Brittain, Vera. Account Rendered. Macmillan. $3
Bromfield, Louis. The Wild Country. Harper. $2.75
Bruller, Jean. Silence of the Sea. Macmillan. $1
* Cabell, James B. The Devil's Own Dear Son. Farrar. $2.75
† Cadell, Elizabeth. Iris in Winter. Morrow. $3
Cary, Joyce. Herself Surprised. Harper. $3
*† Cather, Willa S. Song of the Lark. Houghton. $3.50
Chamberlain, George. Knoll Island. Bobbs. $2.50
† ——— Midnight Boy. Bobbs. $2.75
Chase, Mary Ellen. The Plum Tree. Macmillan. $2

15

Conrad, Joseph. The Conrad Argosy. Doubleday.
Cooper, Louise F. Deer on the Stairs. Duell. $2.50
† Davies, Valentine. It Happens Every Spring. Farrar. $2.50.
† ———— Miracle on 34th Street. Harcourt. $1.75
* de Vilmorin, Louise. Erica's Return. Random. $2.50
Dever, Joseph. No Lasting Home. Bruce. $3
Dick, R. A. Ghost and Mrs. Muir. Ziff-Davis. $2
Dos Passos, John. The Grand Design. Houghton. $3.50
Douglas, Lloyd. Disputed Passage. Houghton. $3
———— Dr. Hudson's Secret Journal. Houghton. $2.75
———— Green Light. Houghton. $3
———— Invitation to Live. Houghton. $2.75
† Edwards, Edward J. The Chosen. Longmans. $3
† Field, Rachel. And Now Tomorrow. Macmillan. $3
Fisher, Vardis. April. Caxton. $2
Fletcher, Harry L. V. Woman's House. Messner. $2.75
Friedlander, Mort. The Yellow Leaf. Wyn. $2
Friesen, Gordon. Flamethrowers. Caxton. $3.50
Goertz, Arthémise. Give Us Our Dream. McGraw. $2.75
Hall, James N. Lost Island. Little. $2
Hayes, Alfred. The Girl on the Via Flaminia. Harper. $2.50
Hemingway, Ernest. A Farewell to Arms. Scribner. $6.50
Hergesheimer, Joseph. Bright Shawl. Knopf. $2.50
* ———— Three Black Pennys. Knopf. $3.50
Higginbotham, Robert E. Wine for My Brothers. Rinehart. $2.50
Hughes, Dorothy B. The Big Barbecue. Random. $2.75
Hughes, Richard. The Innocent Voyage. Heritage. $3.75
Jordan, Helen R. Lost Captain. Dodd. $3
* Kafka, Franz. Metamorphosis. Vanguard. $2.75
Kafka, John. Sicilian Street. Coward. $3
† Kahmann, Chesley. Gypsy Melody. Random. $2.50
Kendrick, Baynard. The Tunnel. Scribner. $3
Koestler, Arthur. Arrival and Departure. Macmillan. $2.75
Lagerlöf, Selma. Liliecrona's Home. Dutton. $2.50

Laski, Marghanita. Toasted English. Houghton. $2.50

*† Laverty, Maura. Never No More. Longmans. $2.50

Lawson, Robert. Mr. Wilmer. Little. $2.50

Lea, Tom. The Brave Bulls. Little. $3

† Lehmann, Rosamond. Dusty Answer. Harcourt. $2.50

Leonov, Leonid. Chariot of Wrath. Wyn. $2.50.

† Lyon, Jessica. For a Whole Lifetime. Macrae. $2.50

Maugham, Somerset. Catalina. Doubleday. $3

Merrick, Elliott. Frost and Fire. Scribner. $3

Milne, Alan A. Mr. Pim. Dutton. $2.50

Moorhead, Alan. Rage of the Vultures. Scribner. $3

Nathan, Robert. The River Journey. Knopf. $2.50

† Obermeyer, Rosemary. Golden Apples of the Sun. Dutton. $2.75.

O'Donnell, Mary K. Those Other People. Houghton. $2.50

† O'Neal, Charles. Three Wishes of Jamie McRuin. Messner. $2.75

Paine, Ralph D. College Years. Scribner. $2

Panova, Vera. The Train. Knopf. $3.

Partridge, Bellamy. The Old Oaken Bucket. Crowell. $3

Purcell, Patrick. The Quiet Man. Putnam. $2.50

Quigley, Martin. A Tent on Corsica. Lippincott. $2.75

Ramuz, Charles F. When the Mountain Fell. Pantheon Books. $2.50

Scannell, Francis P. In Line of Duty. Harper. $2.50

† Scholz, Jackson V. Johnny King, Quarterback. Morrow. $2.50

Simonov, Konstantine. Days and Nights. Simon. $2.75

Slater, Humphrey. Conspirator. Harcourt. $2.50

Smith, Carmichael. Atomsk. Duell. $2.50

Spalding, Helen. The White Witnesses. Scribner. $3

Spewack, Samuel. Busy, Busy People. Houghton. $3

Stegner, Wallace. Second Growth. Houghton. $2.75

*† Steinbeck, John. The Pearl. Viking. $2

———— Tortilla Flat. Viking. $6

Stern, David. Francis Goes to Washington. Farrar. $2.75

† Stewart, George R. Fire. Random. $3

Stone, Irving. Passionate Journey. Doubleday. $3

17

Strauss, Theodore. Moonrise. Viking. $2.50

Stuart, Jesse. Taps for Private Tussie. Dutton. $3.75

Sumner, Cid R. But the Morning Will Come. Bobbs. $3

Taunay, Alfredo D'E. Inocencia. Macmillan. $2.50

Taylor, Elizabeth. Wreath of Roses. Knopf. $3

* Tchkotoua, Prince Nicholas. Timeless. Murray & Gee. $3

† Thane, Elswyth. Kissing Kin. Duell. $3

———— The Tryst. Duell. $2.75

Thruelsen, Richard, and Arnold, Elliott. Mediterranean Sweep. Duell. $3

Train, Arthur. Paper Profits. Liveright. $3

Vailland, Roger. Play for Keeps. Houghton. $3

Verissimo, Erico. Consider the Lilies of the Field. Macmillan. $3

———— The Rest Is Silence. Macmillan. $3

Vidal, Gore. In a Yellow Wood. Dutton. $2.75

Wakeman, Frederic. The Wastrel. Rinehart. $2.75

Walker, Mannix. Magnolia Widow. Dodd. $3

Walker, Mildred. Medical Meeting. Harcourt. $3

———— Unless the Wind Turns. Harcourt. $2

Waugh, Evelyn. Scott King's Modern Europe. Little. $2

West, Keith. Winter Cherry. Macmillan. $2

White, Max. Man Who Carved Women from Wood. Harper. $3

Williams, Charles. Many Dimensions. Pellegrini. $3

Williamson, Thames. Christine Roux. Wyn. $2.50

Wouk, Herman. Aurora Dawn. Simon. $2.75

PORTRAITS OF PEOPLE

Collected Biography

Beard, Annie. Our Foreign Born Citizens. Crowell. $2.50

† Bolton, Sarah K. Lives of Girls Who Became Famous. Crowell. $2.75

Booth, Edward T. Country Life in America, as Lived by Ten Presidents of the United States. Knopf. $3.75

Bradford, Gamaliel. As God Made Them: Portraits of Some Nineteenth Century Americans. Houghton. $4
———— The Quick and the Dead. Houghton. $4
Cunningham, Eugene. Triggernometry. Caxton. $4.50
Dies, Edward J. Titans of the Soil: Great Builders of Agriculture. Univ. of North Carolina Press. $3.50
Guedalla, Philip. Bonnet and Shawl. Putnam. $3.50
† Hamilton, Elizabeth B., ed. How They Started. Harcourt. $2.50
Holbrook, Stewart H. Lost Men of American History. Macmillan. $4
Kuo, Helen. Giants of China. Dutton. $3
Young, Klyde H., and Middleton, Lamar. Heirs Apparent: The Vice Presidents of the United States. Prentice-Hall. $3.75

Individual Biography

Alsop, Gulielma F. Deer Creek: A Golden Childhood. Vanguard. $3
† Anthony, Katharine S. Queen Elizabeth. Knopf. $2.50
Antin, Mary. Promised Land. Houghton. $3
Baker, Louise. Out on a Limb. McGraw. $2
† Baker, Rachel. First Woman Doctor: The Story of Elizabeth Blackwell, M.D. Messner. $2.75
Bauer, Harold. Harold Bauer, His Book. Norton. $3.75
Beatty, Richmond C. Lord Macaulay. Univ. of Oklahoma Press. $3
Bellah, James W. Irregular Gentleman. Doubleday. $3
Berryman, Opal L. Pioneer Preacher. Crowell. $3
† Bick, Christopher. Bells of Heaven. Dodd. $3
Biddle, Francis. Mr. Justice Holmes. Scribner. $3
Bingay, Malcolm W. Of Me I Sing. Bobbs. $3.50
Boardman, Philip. Patrick Geddes. Univ. of North Carolina Press. $5
Boehmer, Heinrich. Road to Reformation. Muhlenberg Press. $4
Bowen, Louise de K. Open Windows. Seymour. $2.50
Bretz, Alice. I Begin Again. McGraw. $2
Brimlow, George F. Cavalryman out of the West. Caxton. $5
Burbank, Luther. Harvest of the Years. Houghton. $2.50
Burgess, Perry. Who Walk Alone. Holt. $2.75

Burlingame, Roger. Whittling Boy: The Story of Eli Whitney. Harcourt. $3

* Burton, Jean. Lydia Pinkham Is Her Name. Farrar. $2.75

Burton, Katherine. The Next Thing. Longmans. $3

Butler, Nicholas M. Across the Busy Years. Scribner. 2v. $3.75 ea.

Byers, Tracy. Martha Berry. Putnam. $3.75

Campbell, Sir Gerald. Of True Experience. Dodd. $3.50

† Carmichael, Hoagland. Stardust Road. Rinehart. $2

Carnegie, Andrew. Autobiography. Houghton. $2

Case, Frank. Tales of a Wayward Inn. Lippincott. $3.50

Cecil, David. Two Quiet Lives. Bobbs. $3

† Chamberlain, Henriqueta. Where the Sabia Sings. Macmillan. $3

Chanler, Margaret. Memory Makes Music. Greenberg. $2.50

Chase, Mary Ellen. Goodly Fellowship. Macmillan. $3

Chesterton, Gilbert K. St. Thomas Aquinas. Sheed. $2.75

Chevigny, Hector. My Eyes Have a Cold Nose. Yale Univ. Press. $3.50

Cook, Reginald L. Passage to Walden. Houghton. $3

Corle, Edwin. John Studebaker: An American Dream. Dutton. $4.50

Corrigan, Douglas. That's My Story. Dutton. $1.50

† Courtney, Charles. Unlocking Adventure: The Autobiography of a World-famous Locksmith. McGraw. $3.50

Croy, Homer. Jesse James Was My Neighbor. Duell. $3.50

Crumbine, Samuel J. Frontier Doctor. Dorrance. $3

† Dahl, Borghild M. I Wanted To See. Macmillan. $2.50

Daniel, Hawthorne. End of Track. Caxton. $3

† Day, Clarence. Life with Father. Knopf. $2

Day, Richard E. Breakfast Table Autocrat. Moody Press. $3

Dinneen, Joseph F. The Purple Shamrock: The Hon. James Michael Curley of Boston. Norton. $3.75

Dorsey, Florence. Road to the Sea: The Story of James B. Eads. Rinehart. $4

Dows, Olin. Franklin Roosevelt at Hyde Park. American Artists' Group. $5

Drooz, Irma G. Doctor of Medicine. Dodd. $3

Eastman, Max. Enjoyment of Living. Harper. $5

Eaton, Evelyn. Every Month Was May. Harper. $2.75

———— North Star Is Nearer. Rinehart. $2.75

† Eaton, Jeanette. A Daughter of the Seine: The Life of Madame Roland. Harper. $1.40

† ———— Leader by Destiny: George Washington, Man and Patriot. Harcourt. $3.50

Elias, Robert H. Theodore Dreiser. Knopf. $4

Ernst, Morris L. So Far So Good. Harper. $3

Evans, Jean. Chateaubriand. Macmillan. $3.10

Fairchild, David. The World Grows Round My Door. Scribner. $5

* Flake, Arthur. Life at Eighty as I See It. Broadman. $1.25

* Fries, Ulrich S. From Copenhagen to Okonogan: The Autobiography of a Pioneer. Caxton. $5

Frothingham, Thomas G. Washington, Commander in Chief. Houghton. $5

Ghéon, Henri. St. Martin of Tours. Sheed. $2.25

Girdler, Tom M. Boot Straps. Scribner. $4

*† Goss, Madeleine. Beethoven, Master Musician. Holt. $3

† ———— Deep-flowing Brook, the Life of Johann Sebastian Bach. Holt. $3

Gould, R. E. Yankee Storekeeper. Grosset. $1

† Graham, Frank. Lou Gehrig, a Quiet Hero. Putnam. $2.50

* Green, James A. William Henry Harrison, His Life and Times. Kidd. $5

Griggs, Edward H. Story of an Itinerant Teacher. Bobbs. $1.50

Hagedorn, Hermann. Roosevelt in the Bad Lands. Houghton. $2.50

Haley, J. Evetts. Charles Goodnight: Cowman and Plainsman. Univ. of Oklahoma Press. $5

Hanna, Alfred J. Prince in Their Midst: The Adventurous Life of Achille Murat on the American Frontier. Univ. of Oklahoma Press. $3

Harding, Bertita. Lost Waltz. Bobbs. $3.50

Harris, Seale. Banting's Miracle: The Story of the Discovery of Insulin. Lippincott. $3.50

Hart, Ivor B. James Watt and the History of Steam Power. Schuman. $4

Harvey, Ruth. Curtain Time. Houghton. $3

Hatch, Alden. Young Willkie. Harcourt. $2.50

Hathaway, Katherine B. Journals and Letters of the Little Locksmith. Coward. $3.75

Hedman, Martha. Uncle, Aunt and Jezebel. Scribner. $3

Helm, MacKinley. Angel Mo' and Her Son, Roland Hayes. Little. $3

Higginbottom, Sam. Sam Higginbottom, Farmer. Scribner. $3

Hines, Jack. Minstrel of the Yukon. Greenberg. $2.75

Hodges, C. Walter. Columbus Sails. Coward. $3

Hopkins, Mary A. Hannah More and Her Circle. Longmans. $3.50

Ireland, Alleyne. An Adventure with a Genius. Dutton. $3

Jannopoulo, Helen P. And across Big Seas. Caxton. $5

Johnson, Gerald W. First Captain, the Story of John Paul Jones. Coward. $3.50

———— Liberal's Progress. Coward. $3.50

Kantor, MacKinlay. But Look, the Morn. Coward. $3.50

Karr, Jean. Grace Livingston Hill, Her Story and Her Writings. Greenberg. $2.50

* Keithley, Ralph. Buckey O'Neill. Caxton. $3.50

Kimbrough, Emily. How Dear to My Heart. Grosset. $1.49

† Linduska, Noreen. My Polio Past. Pellegrini. $2.75

Lloyd, John A. T. Fyodor Dostoevsky. Scribner. $3.50

Long, Eugene H. O. Henry: The Man and His Works. Univ. of Pennsylvania Press. $2.75

Lonyay, Count Carl. Rudolph: The Tragedy of Mayerling. Scribner. $5

† Louis, Joe. My Life Story. Duell. $2.75

Lubbock, Percy. Portrait of Edith Wharton. Appleton. $3

McDermott, Thomas. Keeper of the Keys: A Life of Pope Pius XII. Bruce. $2.50

McDowell, Amanda, and Blankenship, L. M. Fiddles in the Cumberlands. Richard R. Smith. $3

* McIntire, Ross T. White House Physician. Putnam. $3

† Malvern, Gladys. Curtain Going Up! The Story of Katharine Cornell. Messner. $2.75

———— Dancing Star (Pavlova). Messner. $2.75

Mansfield, Katherine. Journal. Knopf. $4

———— Scrapbook. Knopf. $2.50

Marshall, Katherine T. Together: The Annals of an Army Wife. Tupper and Love. $3.50

* Mauldin, Bill. Back Home. Sloane. $3.50

* ———— A Sort of Saga. Sloane. $3.50

Maurois, André. From My Journal. Harper. $2.75

Meadowcroft, William H. Boy's Life of Edison. Harper. $2

Mellor, William B. Patton, Fighting Man. Putnam. $3

Mencken, Henry L. The Days of H. L. Mencken. Knopf. $4.50

Menjou, Adolphe. It Took Nine Tailors. McGraw. $4

Meyer May, Jacques. Siam Doctor. Garden City. $2.75

Muir, John. Story of My Boyhood and Youth. Houghton. $3

Munthe, Axel. The Story of San Michele. Dutton. $4.50

Neagoë, Peter. A Time to Keep. Coward. $3

Neff, Emery. Edwin Arlington Robinson. Sloane. $3.50

Newcomb, Corvelle. Larger Than the Sky: A Story of James Cardinal Gibbons. Longmans. $2.75

Nock, Albert J. Henry James. Morrow. $2.50

Noyes, Pierrepont B. My Father's House: An Oneida Boyhood. Rinehart. $3.50

Odlum, Hortense. A Woman's Place. Scribner. $2.75

Oliver, Simeon, and Hatch, Alden. Back to the Smoky Seas. Messner. $2.75

Ossendowski, Ferdinand A. Lenin, God of the Godless. Dutton. $5

Paisley, Eva W. Sanctuary. Dutton. $3

Palencia, Isabel de. Alexandra Kollontay, Ambassadress from Russia. Longmans. $3.50

† Papashvily, George, and Papashvily, Helen. Anything Can Happen. Harper. $2

† Partridge, Bellamy. Big Family. McGraw. $3

Peattie, Donald C. Road of a Naturalist. Houghton. $3.50

Perénye, Eleanor. More Was Lost. Little. $2.75

Pinkerton, Kathrene. Two Ends to Our Shoestring. Harcourt. $2.75

Plagemann, Bentz. My Place to Stand. Farrar. $2.75

Plass, Ewald. This Is Luther. Concordia. $5

Poor, Charles. Goya. Scribner. $5

* Puner, Helen W. Freud, His Life and His Mind. Crown. $4

Putnam, George P. Soaring Wings: A Biography of Amelia Earhart. Harcourt. $2.50

Reyher, Rebecca H. Zulu Woman. Columbia Univ. Press. $3

Richardson, Henry Handel. Myself When Young. Norton. $3

Rodney, George B. As a Cavalryman Remembers. Caxton. $4

Roosevelt, Eleanor. This I Remember. Harper. $4

Roosevelt, Franklin D. F. D. R., His Personal Letters. Duell. $5

† Rourke, Constance. Audubon. Harcourt. $2.69

† ——— Davy Crockett. Harcourt. $2.75

Ruggles, Eleanor. Journey into Faith: The Anglican Life of John Henry Newman. Norton. $4

† Russell, Harold. Victory in My Hands. Creative Age. $2.50

Sagendorph, Kent. Stevens Thomson Mason. Dutton. $4.75

† Schweitzer, Albert. Memoirs of Childhood and Youth. Macmillan. $1.75

† Seagrave, Gordon S. Burma Surgeon. Norton. $3

Sedgwick, Ellery. Happy Profession. Little. $3.50

Sheean, Vincent. Lead, Kindly Light. Random. $2.50

† Sheerin, Maria W. Parson Takes a Wife. Macmillan. $2.75

Shridharani, Krishnalal J. The Mahatma and the World. Duell. $3.50

Shumway, Harry I. Bernard M. Baruch. Page. $1.25

——— Lawrence, the Arabian Knight. Page. $2

Sikorsky, Igor I. Story of the Winged-S. Dodd. $4

Sissons, Constance K. John Kerr. Oxford Univ. Press. $3

Sitwell, Sir Osbert. Great Morning. Little. $4

† Skinner, Cornelia O. Family Circle. Houghton. $3.50

* Stark, Mabel, and Orr, Gertrude. Hold That Tiger. Caxton. $2.50

† Strachey, Lytton. Elizabeth and Essex. Harcourt. $2.29

Stolee, Ingeborg. Luther's Life. Augsburg. $2.50

Strong, Isobel O. This Life I've Loved. Longmans. $3.50

Stuart, Jesse. The Thread That Runs So True. Scribner. $3

Sullivan, John W. N. Isaac Newton, 1642-1727. Macmillan. $3

* Sumner, Francis B. Life History of an American Naturalist. Jaques
    Cattell. $3

Taber, Gladys. The Book of Stillmeadow. Macrae. $3

* Tappan, Eva M. American Hero Stories. Houghton. $2.50

Taylor, Rosemary. Ridin' the Rainbow. McGraw. $2.50

† Teale, Edwin W. Dune Boy. Dodd. $3

† Thane, Elswyth. Tudor Wench. Duell. $2.75

Thomas, Jean. Singin' Fiddler of Lost Hope. Dutton. $3

Thornton, Willis K. Nine Lives of Citizen Train. Greenberg. $3.50

Tillotson, Harry S. Beloved Spy: The Life and Loves of Major John
    André. Caxton. $3.50

Tomlinson, Irving C. Twelve Years with Mary Baker Eddy. Chris-
    tian Science Pub. House. $3

Topp, Mildred S. Smile Please. Houghton. $3.50

Troyat, Henry. Firebrand: The Life of Dostoevsky. Roy. $3.75

Truax, Sarah. A Woman of Parts. Longmans. $3.50

Tully, Grace G. F. D. R., My Boss. Scribner. $3.50

Tyler, Parker. Chaplin, Last of the Clowns. Vanguard. $3

Underwood, Agness. Newspaperwoman. Harper. $3.50

Van Doren, Mark. Nathaniel Hawthorne. Sloane. $3.50

† Van Straaten, Jan. Slavonic Rhapsody. Allen, Towne and Heath.
    $2.75

† Vestal, Stanley. Jim Bridger, Mountain Man. Morrow. $3.50

Wagenknecht, Edward, ed. Joan of Arc: An Anthology of History
    and Literature. Creative Age. $4.50

Walsh, James E. Tales of Xavier. Sheed. $2.50

Waltz, George H., Jr. Jules Verne: The Biography of an Imagination. Holt. $2.50

* Wanless, Lillian E. Wanless of India. Wilde. $3

Weiner, Edward. The Damon Runyon Story. Longmans. $3

Williams, Gertrude M. Priestess of the Occult: Madame Blavatsky. Knopf. $3.50

Williams, Wythe. The Tiger of France: Conversations with Clemenceau. Duell. $4.50

Wilson, Philip. General Evangeline Booth of the Salvation Army. Scribner. $3.50

Winsten, Stephen. Days with Bernard Shaw. Vanguard. $3.75

Wise, James W. Legend of Louise: The Life Story of Mrs. Stephen S. Wise. Jewish Opinion Pub. Corp. $2

† Wood, Laura N. Raymond L. Ditmars: His Exciting Career with Reptiles, Animals and Insects. Messner. $2.75

Woodgate, Mildred V. Abbé Edgeworth. Longmans. $2.50

Woodward, William E. Gift of Life. Dutton. $4.75

Wright, Frank L. Genius and Mobocracy. Duell. $5

Yost, Edna. Frank and Lillian Gilbreth. Rutgers Univ. Press. $5

OUR YESTERYEARS

Our American Heritage

Adams, Brooks. America's Economic Supremacy. Harper. $2.50

Adams, James T. Epic of America. Little. $4

Adams, Randolph G. Pilgrims, Indians, and Patriots. Little. $3

Allen, William R. Chequemegon. William-Frederick Press. $3

Anderson, Frank M. Mystery of "A Public Man": A Historical Detective Story. Univ. of Minnesota Press. $3.75

Bakeless, John. Lewis and Clark. Morrow. $5

Beal, Merrill D. Story of Man in Yellowstone. Caxton. $5

Bill, Alfred H. Rehearsal for Conflict: The War with Mexico. Knopf. $4.50

Blackford, Susan L., comp. Letters from Lee's Army. Scribner. $3.50

Bowers, Claude G. The Party Battles of the Jackson Period. Houghton. $5

* Brown, Henry C. From Alley Pond to Rockefeller Center. Dutton. $4.25

Chaffin, Lorah B. Sons of the West. Caxton. $3

Coleman, Roy V. The First Frontier. Scribner. $3.75

Coolidge, Dane. Old California Cowboys. Dutton. $3

Cruse, Thomas. Apache Days and After. Caxton. $3.50

Daniels, Josephus. The Wilson Era. 2v. Univ. of North Carolina Press. $4 ea.

DeForest, John W. A Union Officer in the Reconstruction. Yale Univ. Press. $3.75

Dobie, J. Frank. Apache Gold and Yaqui Silver. Little. $4.50

——— Longhorns. Little. $4

Drury, John. Midwest Heritage. Wyn. $5

Emrich, Duncan. It's an Old Wild West Custom. Vanguard. $3

Foreman, Grant. Last Trek of the Indians. Univ. of Chicago Press. $5

Fougera, Katherine G. With Custer's Cavalry. Caxton. $3

Hoad, Louise G. Kickapoo Indian Trails. Caxton. $2.50

Holbrook, Stewart H. Iron Brew: A Century of American Ore and Steel. Macmillan. $3

Hugh-Jones, Edward M. Woodrow Wilson and American Liberalism. Macmillan. $2

Isley, Bliss. Blazing the Way West. Scribner. $3.50

Kincaid, Robert L. Wilderness Road. Bobbs. $3.75

Mathews, John J. Wah' Kon-Tah: The Osage and the White Man's Road. Univ. of Oklahoma Press. $2.50

Monaghan, Jay. Overland Trail. Bobbs. $4

Ottley, Roi. Black Odyssey; the Story of the Negro in America. Scribner. $3.50

Peckham, Howard H. Pontiac and the Indian Uprisings. Princeton Univ. Press. $4.50

Pratt, Fletcher. Ordeal by Fire: An Informal History of the Civil War. Sloane. $5

Roosevelt, Theodore. Rough Riders. Scribner. $3

* Royce, Ernest. Burbank among the Indians. Caxton. $5

Santee, Ross. Apache Land. Scribner. $3.50

Smith, Ira R. T., and Morris, J. A. "Dear Mr. President": The Story of Fifty Years in the White House Mail Room. Messner. $3

Starkey, Marion L. The Cherokee Nation. Knopf. $3.50

Stilwell, Joseph W. The Stilwell Papers. Sloane. $4

Wells, Evelyn, and Peterson, Harry C. The '49ers. Doubleday. $3

White, William Allen. Changing West. Macmillan. $1.50

Winther, Oscar O. The Great Northwest. Knopf. $4.50

———— Via Western Express and Stagecoach. Stanford Univ. Pr. $3

Civilization in Retrospect

Beasley, Norman. Politics Has No Morals. Scribner. $3

Beecher, John. All Brave Sailors: The Story of the S. S. Booker T. Washington. Wyn. $2.50

Botsford, George W. Hellenic History. Macmillan. $6

Burney, Christopher. Dungeon Democracy. Duell. $2

Capa, Robert. Slightly out of Focus. Holt. $3.50

Chaplin, William W. Seventy Thousand Miles of War. Appleton. $3

Chronicles of America. 50v. Yale Univ. Press. Various editions.

Cleveland, Reginald M. Air Transport at War. Harper. $3.50

Davies, Raymond A. Odyssey Through Hell. Wyn. $2

De Guingand, Sir Francis. Operation Victory. Scribner. $3.75

De Pury, Roland. Journal from My Cell. Harper. $1.50

Dilts, Marion M. Pageant of Japanese History. Longmans. $4

Fischer, Louis. Gandhi and Stalin. Harper. $2

Foltz, Charles, Jr. Masquerade in Spain. Houghton. $4

Foote, Alexander. Handbook for Spies. Doubleday. $2.50

Gentile, Don S., and Wolfert, Ira. One Man Air Force. Wyn. $1.25

Gibbon, Edward. Decline and Fall of the Roman Empire. 3v. Heritage. $17.50

Gruber, Ruth. Destination Palestine. Wyn. $2.50

Haas, William S. Iran. Columbia Univ. Press. $3.50

Hamilton, James W., and Bolce, William J., Jr. Gateway to Victory. Stanford Univ. Press. $3

Harper, Frank. Night Climb: The Story of the Skiing 10th. Longmans. $2.50

Henderson, Daniel. From the Volga to the Yukon. Hastings House. $3

Hirschmann, Ira A. Life Line for a Promised Land. Vanguard. $3

Kelley, Douglas M. 22 Cells in Nuremberg: A Psychiatrist Examines the Nazi Criminals. Greenberg. $3

King, William B., and O'Brien, Frank. The Balkans, Frontier of Two Worlds. Knopf. $3.50

Koriakov, Mikhail. I'll Never Go Back: A Red Army Officer Talks. Dutton. $3

Lamb, Harold. The City and the Tsar: Peter the Great and the Move to the West. Doubleday. $4.50

Larsen, Karen. A History of Norway. Princeton Univ. Press. $6

Lawrence, Thomas E. Seven Pillars of Wisdom. Doubleday. $5

Lindbergh, Charles A. Of Flight and Life. Scribner. $1.50

Long, Haniel. The Power within Us: Cabeza de Vaca's Relation of His Journey from Florida to the Pacific, 1528-1536. Duell. $2

Ludwig, Emil. July '14. Putnam. $4

McNeill, William H. The Greek Dilemma: War and Aftermath. Lippincott. $3.50

Marsden, Lawrence A. Attack Transport: The Story of the U. S. S. Doyen. Univ. of Minnesota Press. $2.50

Mather, Rufus G. Excavating Buried Treasure (in Archives). Harvard Univ. Press. $4

Mauldin, William H. Up Front. Holt. $3

Meadowcroft, Enid L. Gift of the River: A History of Ancient Egypt. Crowell. $2.50

Mills, Lenox A., and associates. The New World of Southeast Asia. Univ. of Minnesota Press. $5

Parsons, Geoffrey. Stream of History. Scribner. $5

Patton, George S., Jr. War as I Knew It. Houghton. $4

Peattie, Donald C. Immortal Village. Univ. of Chicago Press. $2.75

Peck, Graham. Through China's Wall. Houghton. $3.50

Reischauer, Edwin O. Japan, Past and Present. Knopf. $2

Roosevelt, Elliot. As He Saw It. Duell. $3

Schuschnigg, Kurt von. Austrian Requiem. Putnam. $3.50

Seeger, Elizabeth. Pageant of Chinese History. Longmans. $3.50

Sforza, Carlo. Contemporary Italy. Dutton. $3.75

Sharon, Henrietta B. It's Good to Be Alive. Dodd. $2

Smith, Goldwin. A History of England. Scribner. $6.75

Soward, Frederic H. Twenty-five Troubled Years, 1918-1943. Oxford Univ. Press. $3

Sternberg, Fritz. How to Stop the Russians Without War. Day. $2

Sturzo, Luigi. Italy and the Coming World. Roy. $3.50

Tenien, Mark. Chungking Listening Post. Creative Age. $2.50

Thornburn, Lois M., and Donaldson, B. No Tumult, No Shouting: The Story of the PBY. Holt. $2.50

Toynbee, Arnold J. Civilization on Trial. Oxford Univ. Press. $3.50

Villiers, Alan. The Coral Sea. McGraw. $4

Welles, Sam. Profile of Europe. Harper. $3.50

Winfield, Gerald F. China, the Land and the People. Sloane. $5

Woodbury, David O. Builders for Battle: How Pacific Naval Air Bases Were Constructed. Dutton. $7.50

Our Neighbors

Andrews, Clarence L. Sitka. Caxton. $3

———— Story of Alaska. Caxton. $4

Barbeau, Charles M. Alaska Beckons. Caxton. $4.50

Farnum, Mabel. Seven Golden Cities. Bruce. $2.75

Jones, Tom B. South America Rediscovered. Univ. of Minnesota Press. $4

King, William L. MacKenzie. Canada and the Fight for Freedom. Duell. $3.50

Monaghan, Forbes. Under the Red Sun: A Letter from Manila. McMullen. $2.75

Munro, Ross. Gauntlet to Overlord: The Story of the Canadian Army. Macmillan. $3.50

Prescott, William H. Conquest of Mexico. Heritage. $5

———— Conquest of Mexico, Designed for Modern Reading. Messner. $5

Shapiro, Harry L. Heritage of the Bounty. Simon. $3

Simpson, L. B. Many Mexicos. Putnam. $3.50

Soljak, Philip L. New Zealand: Pacific Pioneer. Macmillan. $3

Strode, Hudson. Timeless Mexico. Harcourt. $3.50

Van de Water, Frederic F. Lake Champlain and Lake George. Bobbs. $4

Warren, Harris G. Paraguay. Univ. of Oklahoma Press. $5

Wrong, George M. The Canadians. Macmillan. $4

Historic Rivers and Lakes

Coffin, Robert P. T. Kennebec, Cradle of Americans. Rinehart. $3

Dan, Julian. Sacramento, River of Gold. Rinehart. $3

Daniels, Jonathan. Frontier on the Potomac. Macmillan. $3

Dryden, Cecil. Up the Columbia for Furs. Caxton. $4

Gray, James. The Illinois. Rinehart. $3

Hansen, Harry. The Chicago. Rinehart. $3.50

Hatcher, Harlan. Lake Erie. Bobbs. $4

Havighurst, Walter. Long Ships Passing. Macmillan. $3.50

———— Upper Mississippi. Rinehart. $3

Hinkle, George, and Hinkle, Bliss. Sierra-Nevada Lakes. Bobbs. $4

Landon, Fred. Lake Huron. Bobbs. $4

Minter, J. E. The Chagres. Rinehart. $4

Nute, Grace L. Lake Superior. Bobbs. $4

Pound, Arthur. Lake Ontario. Bobbs. $4

Roberts, Leslie. The Mackenzie. Rinehart. $3.50

Wilson, William E. The Wabash. Rinehart. $3

Our Cities and Our States

Altrocchi, Julia C. The Spectacular San Franciscans. Dutton. $4.50

Beal, Merrill D. History of Southeastern Idaho. Caxton. $3

Beston, Henry. Northern Farm: A Chronicle of Maine. Rinehart. $3

Bickel, Karl A. The Mangrove Coast. Coward. $3

Blegen, Theodore C. Grass Roots History. Univ of Minnesota Press. $3

Blegen, Theodore C., and Jordan, Philip. With Various Voices. Itasca Press. $5

Cameron, Marguerite. This Is the Place. Caxton. $3

Carmer, Carl. Dark Trees to the Wind. Sloane. $3.75

Chambrun, Clara L. Comtesse de. Cincinnati: The Story of the Queen City. Scribner. $3.75

Garwood, Darrell. Crossroads of America: The Story of Kansas City. Norton. $3.75

Gittinger, Roy. The Formation of the State of Oklahoma. Univ. of Oklahoma Press. $2.50

Hancock, Ralph. Fabulous Boulevard. Funk. $3.50

Jennings, John. Boston, Cradle of Liberty, 1630-1776. Doubleday. $3.50

Kane, Harnett. Natchez on the Mississippi. Morrow. $5

McIlwaine, Shields. Memphis Down in Dixie. Dutton. $4.50

MacMullen, Jerry. Paddle-Wheel Days in California. Stanford Univ. Press. $3

Mitchell, Edwin V. It's an Old Cape Cod Custom. Vanguard. $3

—— It's an Old New England Custom. Vanguard. $3

—— It's an Old Pennsylvania Custom. Vanguard. $3

—— It's an Old State of Maine Custom. Vanguard. $3

Mora, Jo. Californios, the Saga of the Hard-riding Vaqueros, America's First Cowboys. Doubleday. $3.75

Nelson, Bruce. Land of the Dacotahs. Univ. of Minnesota Press. $3.75

Robinson, Lura. It's an Old New Orleans Custom. Vanguard. $3

Rollinson, John K. Wyoming Cattle Trails. Caxton. $5
Shippey, Lee. It's an Old California Custom. Vanguard. $3
Smith, Marion J. A History of Maine. Falmouth Pub. $5
West, Ray B., Jr., ed. Rocky Mountain Cities. Norton. $4

THIS EARTH, THIS REALM

America, America

* Allen, Eleanor. Canvas Caravans. Binfords and Mort. $2.50
Almirall, Leon V. Canines and Coyotes. Caxton. $3
Arnold, Oren. Sun in Your Eyes. Univ. of New Mexico Press. $2.50
Brown, Rollo. I Travel by Train. Appleton. $3
Caen, Herberg E. Baghdad-by-the-Bay. Doubleday. $3.50
Carmer, Carl. The Hudson. Rinehart. $3
Coatsworth, Elizabeth. Country Neighborhood. Macmillan. $2.50
Coffin, Robert T. Mainstays of Maine. Macmillan. $2.50
———— Yankee Coast. Macmillan. $4
Crosby, Katherine. Blue-Water Men and Other Cape Codders.
    Macmillan. $3.50
Early, Eleanor. Cape Cod Summer. Houghton. $3
Frank, Waldo. The Re-discovery of America: and, Chart for Rough
    Waters. Duell. $5
Hark, Ann. Hex Marks the Spot. Lippincott. $3
Hibben, Frank C. Lost Americans. Crowell. $2.50
Higman, Harry W., and Larrison, Earl J. Pilchuck: The Life of a
    Mountain. Superior Pub. $3.50
Howe, Mark A. De W. Boston Landmarks. Hastings House. $2.50
Howland, Llewellyn. Sou'west and by West of Cape Cod. Harvard
    Univ. Press. $3
† Jaques, Florence P. Canoe Country. Univ. of Minnesota Press. $2.50
† ———— Snowshoe Country. Univ. of Minnesota Press. $3
James, Will. Cow Country. Grosset. $1.49
† ———— Cowboys, North and South. Scribner. $2
———— Drifting Cowboys. Scribner. $2.50

Kane, Harnett. Bayous of Louisiana. Morrow. $5

* Leighton, Clare. Southern Harvest. Macmillan. $3.50

* McEwen, Inez P. So This Is Ranching! Caxton. $4

Meier, Frank. Hurricane Warning. Dutton. $3.50

*† Mora, Joseph J. Trail Dust and Saddle Leather. Scribner. $3.75

O'Shea, Beth. Long Way from Boston. McGraw. $3

† Parkman, Francis. The Oregon Trail. Heritage. $3.75

Peattie, Roderick. Berkshires. Vanguard. $5

———— Sierra Nevada. Vanguard. $5

* Perry, Clay. New England's Buried Treasure. Stephen Daye. $3.50

Peyton, Green. San Antonio, City in the Sun. McGraw. $3.75

Roberts, Kenneth. Trending into Maine. Doubleday. $3.95

Robinson, Bernice N. Winter Harbor. Holt. $2.50

Rutledge, Archibald. God's Children. Bobbs. $3

* ———— Home by the River. Bobbs. $3

* Scott, A. W. Romance of the Highways of California. Griffin-Patterson Co. $3

Snow, Edward R. Mysteries and Adventures along the Atlantic Coast. Dodd. $4

Strunsky, Simeon. No Mean City. Dutton. $3.50

Tallant, Robert. Voodoo in New Orleans. Macmillan. $1.49

Thomas, Jean. Blue Ridge Country. Duell. $3.50

Thorp, Nathan H., and McCullough, Neil. Pardner of the Wind. Caxton. $4

Vreeland, Hamilton, Jr. Twilight of Individual Liberty. Scribner. $2

Whipple, Maurine. This Is the Place: Utah. Knopf. $5

Woodbury, George. John Goffe's Mill. Norton. $3

Arctic to Zanzibar

† Allan, Doug. Gamblers with Fate. McBride. $3

Anderson, Eva G. Dog-Team Doctor. Caxton. $3.50

* Andrews, Roy C. This Business of Exploring. Putnam. $3.50

Arndt, William. From the Nile to the Waters of Damascus. Concordia. $2

Barker, Ernest, ed. Character of England. Oxford Univ. Press. $10

Beaton, Maude H. From Cairo to Khyber to Célebes. Liveright. $3

Birkeland, Joran. Birchland; a Journey Home to Norway. Dutton. $3

* Bone, James. London Echoing. Cape. 18/ **745198**

** Briem, Helgi P. Iceland and the Icelanders. John Francis McKenna Co. $5

Carr, Harry. Old Mother Mexico. Houghton. $3.50

* Cerwin, Herbert. These Are the Mexicans. Harcourt. $5

Chase, Mary Ellen. This England. Macmillan. $2.75

Crow, Carl. Meet the South Americans. Harper. $3

Davies, Blodwen. Gaspé, Land of History and Romance. Greenberg. $4.50

† Diamant, Gertrude. Days of Ofelia. Houghton. $3

Dodge, David. How Lost Was My Week-end. Random. $3

Ehrenburg, Ilya. European Crossroad: A Soviet Journalist in the Balkans. Knopf. $2

Fairchild, David. Garden Islands of the Great East. Scribner. $5

Fergusson, Erna. Venezuela. Knopf. $4

Fergusson, Harvey. Rio Grande. Tudor. $1.98

Gardner, Erle S. The Land of Shorter Shadows. Morrow. $5

Gibbings, Robert. Coming down the Wye. Dutton. $3

———— Lovely Is the Lee. Dutton. $3

———— Over the Reefs and Far Away. Dutton. $3.50

———— Sweet Thames Run Softly. Dutton. $3

Godden, Rumer. Thus Far and No Further. Little. $3

Hanson, Eral P. New Worlds Emerging. Duell. $3.50

Harding, Bertita. The Land Columbus Loved: The Dominican Republic. Coward. $3.75

———— Southern Empire: Brazil. Coward. $4

*† Halliburton, Richard. Glorious Adventure. Garden City. $1

*† ———— New Worlds to Conquer. Garden City. $1

*† ———— Royal Road to Romance. Garden City. $1

*† ———— Seven League Boots. Garden City. $1

35

Herskovits, Melville J., and Herskovits, Frances S. Trinidad Village. Knopf. $4.75

Hinkson, Pamela. Irish Gold. Knopf. $3.50

Ishvani. Brocaded Sari. Day. $2.75

Jaques, Florence P. Canadian Spring. Harper. $3.50

Jewett, A. C. American Engineer in Afghanistan. Univ. of Minnesota Press. $5

Johnson, Martin. Safari. Putnam. $7.50

Kang, Younghill. Grass Roof. Scribner. $3

Karig, Walter. The Fortunate Islands. Rinehart. $3.75

* Keeling, Cecil. Pictures from India. Robert Hale. 15/

† Keith, Agnes N. Land below the Wind. Little. $4

Kinkead, Eugene, and Maloney, Russell. Our Own Baedeker. Simon. $3.75

Knop, Werner. Prowling Russia's Forbidden Zone. Knopf. $2.75

Larralde, Elsa. My House Is Yours. Lippincott. $3

Latourette, Kenneth S. The Chinese, Their History and Culture. Macmillan. $7.50

Levin, Meyer. If I Forget Thee. Viking. $3.50

† Lindbergh, Anne M. Listen! The Wind! Harcourt. $1.49

† ——— North to the Orient. Harcourt. $1.98

Logan, Milla Z. Cousins and Commissars. Scribner. $3

† Lothrop, Eleanor B. Throw Me a Bone. McGraw. $3

McCracken, David R. Four Months on a Jap Whaler. Dodd. $3

* Mitchell, Carleton. Islands to Windward: Cruising the Caribees. Van Nostrand. $12.50

** Montgomery, Doris. Gaspé Coast in Focus. Dutton. $3.50

Morgan, Edward E. P., and Woods, Henry F. God's Loaded Dice: Alaska. Caxton. $4

Muehl, John F. American Sahib. Day. $3

Muir, John. Travels in Alaska. Houghton. $3

Murray, Stuart. Traveler's Guide to France. Sheridan House. $3

Mytinger, Caroline. Headhunting in the Solomon Islands around the Coral Sea. Macmillan. $3

Newman, Bernard. Balkan Background. Macmillan. $2.75

Noice, Harold H. Back of Beyond. Putnam. $3.50

Oakley, Amy, and Oakley, Thornton. Kaleidoscopic Quebec. Appleton. $4

Peattie, Roderick. Struggle on the Veld. Vanguard. $3.50

Petersen, H. Tscherning. Tropical Adventure: Sumatra, Land of Loveliness and Stern Destiny. Roy. $3.50

† Pinkerton, Katherine S. G. Three's a Crew. Grosset. $1.49

Porteus, Stanley D. Calabashes and Kings. Pacific Books. $3.75

Privitera, Joseph F. Latin American Front. Bruce. $2.25

Rama Rau, Santha. Home to India. Harper. $2.50

Raswan, Carl R. Black Tents of Arabia. Creative Age. $3

† Richards, Eva A. Arctic Mood. Caxton. $4

Riddell, James. In the Forests of the Night. A. S. Barnes. $3

Rieseberg, Harry E. Treasure Hunter. Dodd. $3

Romig, Emily C. Pioneer Woman in Alaska. Caxton. $3

* Ronne, Finn. Antarctic Conquest. Putnam. $5

Roosevelt, Theodore. African Game Trails. Scribner. $6

Rothery, Agnes. Iceland, New World Outpost. Viking. $3.75

———— Sweden. Viking. $3

† Scoggin, Margaret C. The Lure of Danger: True Adventure Stories. Knopf. $3

Seabrook, William B. Magic Island. Harcourt. $3.50

Seligman, Adrian. Voyage of the Cap Pilar. Dutton. $4.75

† Small, Marie. Four Fares to Juneau. McGraw. $3

Smith, Nicol. Golden Doorway to Tibet. Bobbs. $3.75

† Stefansson, Evelyn. Within the Circle. Scribner. $2.75

Stefansson, Vilhjalmur. Iceland. Doubleday. $3.50

————, ed. Great Adventures and Explorations. Garden City. $2.49

Tavares de Sá, Hernane. The Brazilians, People of Tomorrow. Day. $3.50

Waln, Nora. Reaching for the Stars. Little. $3.50

† Warner, Esther S. New Songs in a Strange Land. Houghton. $3.50

White, Margaret Bourke-. Halfway to Freedom. Simon. $3.50

Zimmerman, John L. Where the People Sing: Green Land of the Maoris. Knopf. $3

LAUGHTER ABOUNDING

Andrieux, Raymond. Tux 'n Tails. Vanguard. $2.50
Beck, Fred. Second Carrot from the End. Morrow. $2.50
† Becker, May L. Home Book of Laughter. Dodd. $3.50
† Benchley, Robert. Benchley beside Himself. Harper. $2.50
Bennett, Arnold. Buried Alive. Doubleday. $2.50
Brown, John M. Accustomed as I Am. Norton. $2
———— Insides Out. McGraw. $2
Cerf, Bennett A. Try and Stop Me. Simon. $3
Clemens, Samuel L. Adventures of Huckleberry Finn. Heritage. $2.75
———— Adventures of Tom Sawyer. Heritage. $2.75
———— Mysterious Stranger. Harper. $2.50
Denker, Henry. I'll Be Right Home, Ma. Crowell. $2.75
Dickens, Charles. Pickwick Papers. Dodd. $2.75
† Dolson, Hildegarde. We Shook the Family Tree. Random. $2.50
Ethridge, Willie S. It's Greek to Me. Vanguard. $3
Forbes, Kathryn. Mama's Bank Account. Harcourt. $2.25
Franken, Rose. Another Claudia. Rinehart. $2.50
———— Marriage of Claudia. Rinehart. $2.50
Hargrove, Marion. Something's Got to Give. Sloane. $3
Hodgins, Eric. Mr. Blandings Builds His Dream House. Simon. $2.75
Jessel, George. "Hello, Momma." World Pub. $1
Kimbrough, Emily. It Gives Me Great Pleasure. Houghton. $2
† ———— We Followed Our Hearts to Hollywood. Dodd. $2.50
Leacock, Stephen. Last Leaves. Dodd. $2.50
Manners, William. Father and the Angels. Dutton. $2.75
Marquis, Don. . . . Archy and Mehitabel. Doubleday. $2.50
Musselman, Morris M. I Married a Redhead. Crowell. $3

* Perelman, Sidney J. Acres and Pains. Harcourt. $2
———— Keep It Crisp. Garden City. $1
———— Westward Ha! Simon. $2.95
Rorick, Isobel S. Mr. and Mrs. Cugat. Houghton. $2
Rose, Billy. Wine, Women and Words. Simon. $3
Runyon, Damon. Short Takes. McGraw. $3
Saroyan, William. My Name Is Aram. Harcourt. $2.50
† Skinner, Cornelia O. Dithers and Jitters. Dodd. $2
Skinner, Cornelia O., and Kimbrough, Emily. Our Hearts Were
        Young and Gay. Grosset. $1
Streeter, Edward. Father of the Bride. Simon. $2.50
Taylor, Rosemary. Bar Nothing Ranch. McGraw. $3
† Teal, Valentine. It Was Not What I Expected. Duell. $2.75
Thirkell, Angela. August Folly. Knopf. $2.75
———— Summer Half. Knopf. $2.75
Thurber, James. The Beast in Me and Other Animals. Harcourt. $3
———— My World—and Welcome to It. Harcourt. $2.50
Upson, William H. How to Be Rich, Like Me. Little. $2
Westerby, Robert. Champagne for Mother. Duell. $2.50
Wilder, Margaret A. Hurry Up and Wait. McGraw. $2.50

MASKS AND FOOTLIGHTS

† Barrie, James M. Admirable Crichton. Scribner. $2.75
* ———— Boy David. Scribner. $2
———— Dear Brutus. Scribner. $2.75
———— Half Hours and Der Tag. Scribner. $2.50
———— Mary Rose. Scribner. $1.25
———— Quality Street. Scribner. $1.36
———— Shall We Join the Ladies? Scribner. $1.25
———— What Every Woman Knows. Scribner. $2.75
Charsky, Jennie. Persons Lowly Born. Philosophical Library. $3
Claudel, Paul. Three Plays. Humphries. $5
Corwin, Norman. Untitled and Other Radio Dramas. Holt. $3

Drummond, Alexander M., and Gard, Robert E. The Cardiff Giant. Cornell Univ. Press. $2.25

Franken, Rose. Claudia. Rinehart. $2

Kaufman, George S., and Hart, Moss. Six Plays. Random. $1.25

Kingsley, Sidney. Detective Story. Random. $2.50

Koestler, Arthur. Twilight Bar. Macmillan. $2

† Lindsay, Howard, and Crouse, Russel. Clarence Day's Life with Father. Knopf. $3

† ———— . . . Life with Mother. Knopf. $3

McNally, William. Prelude to Exile. Putnam. $2

Mayer, Edwin J. Sunrise in My Pocket: or, The Last Days of Davy Crockett. Messner. $2

Milne, Alan A. The Ivory Door. Putnam. $2.50

———— Toad of Toad Hall. Scribner. $1.50

† Norman, Charles. Playmaker of Avon. McKay. $3

Pirandello, Luigi. As You Desire Me. Dutton. $2.75

Sartre, Jean-Paul. Three Plays. Knopf. $3

* Shakespeare, William. Modern Readers Shakespeare. (Large text with small type notes) Society of Shakesperian Editors. 10v. $12.50

* ———— Plays. (Large text with small type notes) Grosset. $1

As You Like It	Othello
Hamlet	Richard III
Julius Caesar	Romeo and Juliet
Macbeth	Taming of the Shrew
Merchant of Venice	Twelfth Night

Shaw, George Bernard. Six Plays. Dodd. $4.50

Turney, Robert. Daughters of Atreus. Knopf. $2

RHYMES AND RHYTHMS

† Adams, Franklin P. Innocent Merriment. Garden City. $1.49

† Adshead, Gladys L., and Duff, Annis, comps. An Inheritance of Poetry. Houghton. $4

Auden, Wystan H. Collected Poetry. Random. $3.75

Barham, Patricia. Pin-up Poems. Caxton. $2.50

Barker, George. Love Poems. Dial. $2

* Benét, Stephen V. John Brown's Body. Heritage. $5

Benét, William R. Stairway of Surprise. Knopf. $3.50

Bennett, Dorothy. How Strange a Thing. Caxton. $1.50

Berryman, John. The Dispossessed. Sloane. $2.50

Bishop, John P. Collected Poems. Scribner. $4

Bright, Verne. Mountain Men. Caxton. $5

*† Browning, Elizabeth B. Sonnets from the Portuguese. Heritage. o.p.

Browning, Robert. The Ring and the Book. Heritage. o.p.

Campbell, Robert B. The Task. Rinehart. $2

Casey, P. R. Facing West. Caxton. $2

Chaucer, Geoffrey. Canterbury Tales Rendered into Modern English. Garden City. $2.49

———— Canterbury Tales Translated into Modern Verse by F. E.
Hill. Longmans. $3.50

Coates, Grace S. Mead and Mangel-wurzel. Caxton. $2

———— Portulacas in the Wheat. Caxton. $1.50

Coatsworth, Elizabeth. Country Poems. Macmillan. $2.50

———— The Creaking Stair. Coward. $2.75

* Dante Alighieri. Divine Comedy. Heritage. o.p.

de la Mare, Walter. The Burning-Glass and Other Poems. Viking.
$2.50

Engle, Paul. American Child: A Sonnet Sequence. Random. $2

Feeney, Thomas B. When the Wind Blows. Dodd. $2

† Frankel, Elizabeth G. Teen-Age Blues. Messner. $2

Frost, Robert. Complete Poems . . . 1949. Holt. $6

———— New Hampshire. Holt. $2.50

Grelle, Leone R. Country Road. Macmillan. $1.75

Guiterman, Arthur. I Sing the Pioneer. Dutton. $2.25

———— Lyric Laughter. Dutton. $3

Heath-Stubbs, John. Charity of the Stars. Sloane. $2.50

Himmell, Sophie. Spontaneous Now. Fine Editions Press. $2

* Holland, Robert E. The Song of Tekakwitha, the Lily of the Mohawks. Fordham Univ. Press. $2.50

Houselander, Frances Caryll. Flowering Tree. Sheed. $2

Housman, Alfred E. Collected Poems. Holt. $3

Jeffers, Robinson. The Double Axe and Other Poems. Random. $2.75

Karlfeldt, Erik A. Arcadia Borealis. Univ. of Minnesota Press. $3.50

Kipling, Rudyard. A Choice of Kipling's Verse. Scribner. $3

* Lewis, Janet. Earth Bound. Wells College. $4.50

Lincoln, Joseph C. Rhymes of the Old Cape. Appleton. $2.50

Mary Louise, Sister, comp. . . . Over the Bent World. Sheed. $5

Mary Thérèse, Sister. Give Joan a Sword. Macmillan. $1.50

Maynard, Theodore. Collected Poems. Macmillan. $3.50

Meredith, William. Love Letters from an Impossible Land. Yale Univ. Press. $2.50

Merriam, Eve. Family Circle. Yale Univ. Press. $2.50

Merton, Thomas. A Man in the Divided Sea. New Directions. $2.50

Millay, Edna St. V. Collected Lyrics. Harper. 2v. $6

——— Fatal Interview. Harper. $2.25

——— Huntsman What Quarry? Harper. $2

——— Wine from These Grapes. Harper. $2

Morrison, Theodore. Devious Way. Viking. $2

New Poems, 1940, an Anthology of British and American Verse. Yardstick Press. $2.50

* ——— 1942. Peter Pauper Press. $3

Noyes, Alfred. Last Voyage. Lippincott. $2.50

——— Orchard's Bay. (Poetry and essays) Sheed. $2.75

——— Watchers of the Sky. Lippincott. $2.50

Rimbaud, Arthur. Season in Hell. (Parallel French and English texts) New Directions. $1.50

Sarett, Lew R. Slow Smoke. Holt. $2

Sarton, May. The Lion and the Rose. Rinehart. $2

* Shakespeare, William. Sonnets. Heritage. $4.50

Sitwell, Edith. The Song of the Cold. Vanguard. $2.75

Spender, Stephen. The Edge of Being. Random. $2.50

—— Poems of Dedication. Random. $2

Sullivan, John F., Jr. Songs after Sundown. Humphries. $3

* Tate, Allen. The Winter Sea. Cunnington Press. $5

Thompson, Dunstan. Lament for the Sleepwalker. Dodd. $2.50

Virgil. The Aeneid. Heritage. o.p.

Webb, Mary. Fifty-one Poems. Dutton. $2.75

Wolfe, Thomas. Face of a Nation: Poetical Passages. Scribner.
   $2.75

COLLECTED WORKS

NOTE: None of these books are in print, but they have been included because they are in such large, clear print, and most large libraries will have them.

Austen, Jane. Novels and Letters. 12v. Holby

Barrie, James M. Novels, Tales and Sketches. 12v. Scribner

Brontë, Charlotte, and others. Novels of the Sisters Brontë. 12v.
   Thornton ed. John Grant

† Dickens, Charles. Works. 33v. in 20. National Library ed. Bigelow

Eliot, George. Complete Works. 10v. St. James ed. Postlewaite

Fielding, Henry. Works. 6v. Bigelow

Galsworthy, John. Novels, Tales and Plays. 18v. Scribner

Hawthorne, Nathaniel. Works. 10v. Bigelow

Kipling, Rudyard. Works. 13v. Mandalay ed. Doubleday

Lamb, Charles. Life and Works. 8v. Edition de luxe. Brainard

Lincoln, Abraham. Complete Works. 12v. Gettysburg ed. Francis
   D. Tandy

Longfellow, Henry W. Works. 10v. Davos Press

Paine, Thomas. Life and Works. 10v. Thomas Paine National
   Historical Association

Poe, Edgar A. Works. 10v. Scribner

Trollope, Anthony. Barsetshire Novels. 14v. Shakespeare Head ed. Houghton

Turgenieff, Ivan S. Novels and Stories. 16v. Dent

LEISURE-TIME FUN

Indoor Games

Abbott, Jeanne. Fun's Fun. Reilly. $1.50

Culbertson, Ely. Bidding and Playing in Duplicate Contract Bridge. Winston. $2.50

Davidson, H. A. History of Chess. Greenberg. $2.76

duMont, Julius. Basis of Combinations in Chess. McKay. $3

Ellis, Henry M. How to Gain Pleasure and Profit from Stamp Collecting. Funk. $2.75

Leeming, Joseph. Games with Playing Cards. Watts. $2.95

Loso, Foster W. Stamp Collectors' Round Table. Lippincott. $3

MacDougall, Michael. MacDougall on Dice and Cards. Coward. $1.50

North, Robert. Town and Country Games. Crowell. $2.50

Ostrow, Albert A. Complete Card Player. McGraw. $4

Parrish, Robert. New Ways to Mystify. Ackerman. $2

Salzmann, Jerome. The Chess Reader: The Royal Game in World Literature. Greenberg. $5

Outdoor Sports

Bell, W. D. M. Karamojo Safari. Harcourt. $3.75

Boomer, Percy. On Learning Golf. Knopf. $2.75

Bovey, Martin. Whistling Wings. Doubleday. $7.50

Claflin, Bert. Blazed Trails for Anglers. Knopf. $3.50

† Corbett, James E. Man-eaters of Kumaon. Garden City. $1

† ——— The Man-eating Leopard of Rudraprayag. Oxford Univ. Press. $2.50

† Craighead, Frank, and Craighead, John. Hawks in the Hand. Houghton. $3.50

Dalrymple, Byron. Ice-fishing for Everyone. Lantern Press. $3.50
———— Panfish. McGraw. $4.50
Farrington, Selwyn Kip, Jr. The Ducks Came Back. Coward. $5
Fleischer, Nathaniel S. Heavyweight Championship. Putnam. $4.50
Gallico, Paul. Farewell to Sport. Knopf. $2.75
Godfrey, Joseph C., and Dufresne, F., eds. The Great Outdoors. McGraw. $6.50
Haig-Brown, Roderick L. H. A River Never Sleeps. Morrow. $5
Hall, Henry M. A Full Creel. Longmans. $3
Hibben, Frank C. Hunting American Lions. Crowell. $4.50
Hightower, John. Pheasant Hunting. Knopf. $4
Holland, Daniel J. Trout Fishing. Crowell. $5
* Holland, Raymond P. Shotgunning in the Uplands. A. S. Barnes. $7.50
Holland, Robert P., and others. Good Shot! A Book of Rod, Gun and Camera. Knopf. $6
Marshall, Edison. Shikar and Safari. Farrar. $3.50
Moore, Philip H. Castle Buck. Longmans. $3.50
† Powers, James A. Baseball Personalities. Field. $3
Ransom, Elmer. Fishing's Just Luck, and Other Stories. Crown. $2
† Roberts, Howard. The Chicago Bears. Putnam. $3
* Schaldach, William. Coverts and Casts. A. S. Barnes. $5
* ———— Currents and Eddies. A. S. Barnes. $5
Smith, Robert. Baseball. Simon. $3.50
Stilwell, Hart. Fishing in Mexico. Knopf. $4.50
† Stockton, J. Roy. The Gashouse Gang and a Couple of Other Boys. A. S. Barnes. $2.75
*† Tunis, John R. Lawn Games. A. S. Barnes. $1.50
Van de Water, Frederic C. In Defense of Worms and Other Angling Heresies. Duell. $2.50
Wall, Roy. The Contemplative Angler. Putnam. $3.50
** Walton, Izaak. Compleat Angler. Heritage. $5
Wolf, Bill. Reveries of an Outdoor Man. Putnam. $3

EXPLORING SCIENCE

Chase, Carl T. Frontiers of Science. Van Nostrand. $3.75

Cothren, Marion B. This Is the Moon. Coward. $2

Eddington, Sir Arthur. The Expanding Universe. Macmillan. $1.50

Fisk, Dorothy. Exploring the Upper Atmosphere. Oxford Univ. Press. $2

Frost, George E. Planets, Stars and Atoms. Caxton. $3.75

† Harrison, George R. Atoms in Action. Morrow. $5

* Jeans, Sir James. Through Time and Space. Cambridge Univ. Press. $5

Lecomte du Noüy, Pierre. Road to Reason. Longmans. $3.50

Taylor, Frank S. March of the Mind: A Short History of Science. Macmillan. $3.50

Verrill, Alpheus H. Minerals, Metals and Gems. Page. $3.75

† Woodbury, David O. The Glass Giant of Palomar. Dodd. $5

TO YOUR HEALTH!

Bernheim, Bertram M. Medicine at the Crossroads. Morrow. $2.50

Corbett, Margaret D. Help Yourself to Better Sight. Prentice-Hall. $2.50

* Eidelberg, Ludwig. Take Off Your Mask. International Universities Press. $3.50

Freeman, Graydon L., and Stern, Edith M. Mastering Your Nerves. Harper. $2

Galdston, Iago. Progress in Medicine. Knopf. $3

† Garland, Joseph. Story of Medicine. Houghton. $2.75

Harpole, James. Body Menders. Lippincott. $3

Jacobson, Edmund. You Must Relax. McGraw. $2.75

Lieb, Clarence W. Outwitting Your Years. Prentice-Hall. $2.75

Morton, Dudley J. Oh Doctor! My Feet! Appleton. $1.50

Menninger, William C. Psychiatry: Its Evolution and Present Status. Cornell Univ. Press. $2

Rogers, Will. Ether and Me. Putnam. $1.50

Steincrohn, Peter J. What You Can Do for High Blood Pressure. Doubleday. $2.50

Whitman, Armitage. From Head to Foot. Rinehart. $2.50

WORLD HORIZONS

Ascoli, Max. Power of Freedom. Farrar. $2.75

Beals, Carleton. Coming Struggle for Latin America. Lippincott. $3.50

† Bellamy, Francis R. Blood Money: The Story of U. S. Treasury Secret Agents. Dutton. $2.75

Brynes, Asher. Government Against the People. Dodd. $3

Burlingame, Roger. March of the Iron Men: A Social History of Union Through Invention. Scribner. $5

Cabell, James B. Let Me Lie. Farrar. $3.75

* Dallin, David J. Soviet Russia and the Far East. Yale Univ. Press. $5

Dewey, John. Freedom and Culture. Putnam. $2.50

Evatt, Herbert V. The United Nations. Harvard Univ. Press. $2.50

Goble, George W. Design of Democracy. Univ. of Oklahoma Press. $2.75

Huszar, George B. de. Practical Applications of Democracy. Harper. $2

Johnston, Eric. We're All in It. Dutton. $2.75

Jordan, Philip D. The National Road. Bobbs. $4

Kohn, Hans. Prophets and People: Studies in Nineteenth Century Nationalism. Macmillan. $2.75

Kelly, Alfred H., and Harbison, Winfred A. The American Constitution, Its Origin and Development. Norton. $7.50

Lapp, Ralph E. Must We Hide? Addison-Wesley. $3

Latourette, Kenneth S. United States Moves across the Pacific. Harper. $2

Liddell Hart, Basil H. Revolution in Warfare. Yale Univ. Press. $2

Meyer, Cord, Jr. Peace or Anarchy. Little. $2.50

* Nearing, Scott. United World: The Road to International Peace. Island Press. $2.50

Sands, William F., and Lalley, Joseph M. Our Jungle Diplomacy. Univ. of North Carolina Press. $2.50

Timasheff, Nicholas S. Three Worlds: Liberal, Communist and Fascist Society. Bruce. $2.75

Van Loon, Hendrik W. Story of Mankind. Garden City. $1.49

Watkins, Frederic. Political Traditions of the West. Harvard Univ. Press. $5

White, E. B. Wild Flag: Editorials from the *New Yorker* on Federal World Government and Other Matters. Houghton. $2

Wofford, Harris, Jr. It's up to Us: Federal Government in Our Time. Harcourt. $2

FREEDOM'S TORCH

Andrews, Bert. Washington Witch Hunt. Random. $3.50

* Bok, Curtis. Backbone of the Herring. Knopf. $3.50

Bontemps, Arna. Story of the Negro. Knopf. $3

Buaken, Manuel. I Have Lived with the American People. Caxton. $5

Duncan, John A. Strangest Cases on Record. Reilly. $3

Ernst, Morris L. First Freedom. Macmillan. $3

Field, Marshall. Freedom Is More Than a Word. Univ. of Chicago Press. $2.50

Flynn, John T. Epic of Freedom. McKay. $2

† Halsey, Margaret. Color Blind. Simon. $2.50

Hamer, Alvin C., ed. Detroit Murders. Duell. $3

† Harrison, Richard. Scotland Yard. Ziff-Davis. $2.75

Leigh, Robert D., and others. A Free and Responsible Press. Univ. of Chicago Press. $2

Lind, Andrew W. Hawaii's Japanese, an Experiment in Democracy. Princeton Univ. Press. $3

Makris, John N., ed. Boston Murders. Duell. $3

Maritain, Jacques. Rights of Man and Natural Law. Scribner. $2

Meiklejohn, Alexander. Free Speech and Its Relation to Self-government. Harper. $2

Powell, Adam C., Jr. Marching Blacks. Dial. $2.50

Rogge, Oetje J. Our Vanishing Civil Liberties. Gaer. $3

* Safeguarding Civil Liberties Today. Peter Smith. $2.50

Sprigle, Ray. In the Land of Jim Crow. Simon. $2.50

White, William L. Lost Boundaries. Harcourt. $1.50

COUNTRY LIFE

Booth, Edward. God Made the Country. Knopf. $2.50

Clark, William H. Farms and Farmers. Page. $3.75

* Duffus, Robert L. The Valley and Its People: A Portrait of T. V. A. Knopf. $3.50

Fry, Walter, and White, John R. Big Trees. Stanford Univ. Press. $2

Krutch, Joseph. Twelve Seasons: A Perpetual Calendar for the Country. Sloane. $3

Quinn, Vernon. Vegetables in the Garden and Their Legends. Lippincott. $2.50

Salisbury, Edward J. The Living Garden. Macmillan. $3.50

Smith, Newton G. Dahlia Cultivation. Pellegrini. $3.50

Smith, Philip H. Perennial Harvest. Harper. $3

Verrill, Alpheus H. Foods America Gave the World. Page. $3.75

Wilson, Helen V. The African Violet. Barrows. $2.75

TRANSPORTATION—OLD AND NEW

Black, Archibald. Story of Tunnels. McGraw. $2.75

Clark, William H. Railroads and Rivers. Page. $3.75

——— Ships and Sailors. Page. $3.75

Collins, Francis A. Sentinels along Our Coast. Appleton. $2

DuVal, Miles P. And the Mountains Will Move: The Story of the Building of the Panama Canal. Stanford Univ. Press. $5

Farrington, Selwyn Kip, Jr. Railroading from the Rear End. Coward. $5

———— Sport Fishing Boats. Norton. $4

† Floherty, John J. Sons of the Hurricane. Lippincott. $2.50

Gibson, Charles E. The Story of the Ship. Schuman. $4

Hubbard, Freeman H. Railroad Avenue: Great Stories and Legends of American Railroading. McGraw. $3.75

Leyson, Burr. American Wings. Dutton. $2.50

* McNairn, Jack, and MacMullen, Jerry. Ships of the Redwood Coast. Stanford Univ. Press. $3

Zacharoff, Lucien. World's Wings. Duell. $3

COOKBOOKS AND COTTAGES

Brillat-Savarin, Jean A. Physiology of Taste. Heritage. $5

Cobb, Hubbard. Your Dream House: How to Build It for Less Than $3500. Wm. H. Wise. $3.95

Cooper, Virginia M. Creole Kitchen Cook Book. Naylor. $2.50

Draper, Dorothy. Decorating Is Fun. Doubleday. $2.79

Ellsworth, Mary G. Much Depends on Dinner. Knopf. $2

* Hall, Carrie A. From Hoopskirts to Nudity. Caxton. $5

Pepin, Harriet. Fundamentals of Apparel Design. Funk. $5

Platt, June. Party Cookbook. Houghton. $2.75

Stapleton, Elsie. Spending for Happiness. Prentice-Hall. $2.75

Taber, Gladys, and Kistner, Ruth. Flower Arrangement for the American Home. Macrae. $2.75

White, Charles D. Camps and Cottages, How to Build Them. Crowell. $3.50

White, Marion. Mother Hubbard's Cookbook. M. S. Mill. $2

HUMAN DYNAMICS

Adams, Mildred. Getting and Spending. Macmillan. $1

Burlingame, Roger. Backgrounds of Power: The Human Story of Mass Production. Scribner. $6

Burns, Arthur F., and Mitchell, Wesley C. Measuring Business Cycles. National Bureau of Economic Research. $5

Danielian, Noobar R. A. T. and T.: The Story of Industrial Conquest. Vanguard. $3.75

Dillard, Dudley. The Economics of John Maynard Keynes. Prentice-Hall. $5

Goode, Kenneth M., and Kaufman, Zena. Profitable Showmanship. Prentice-Hall. $3

Gregory, Charles O. Labor and the Law. Norton. $5

Haynes, William. Southern Horizons. Van Nostrand. $2.75

Hewes, Thomas. Decentralize for Liberty. Dutton. $3

Kniffen, William H. How to Use Your Bank. McGraw. $3

Laski, Harold J. Trade Unions in the New Society. Viking. $3

Milholland, Ray. Pay Day: Labor and Management in the American System of Free Enterprise. Morrow. $2.50

Ruml, Beardsley. Tomorrow's Business. Farrar. $2.50

Selekman, Benjamin M. Labor Relations and Human Relations. McGraw. $3

Slichter, Sumner H. The Challenge of Industrial Relations, Trade Unions, Management and the Public Interest. Princeton Univ. Press. $2.50

Soule, George. An Economic Constitution for Democracy. Yale Univ. Press. $1.50

Sweezy, Paul M. Socialism. McGraw. $3.50

FINE ART TREASURES

Boswell, Peyton, Jr. Modern American Painting. Dodd. $5.95

Flexner, James T. First Flowers of our Wilderness, American Painting. Houghton. $10

Gradenwitz, Peter. The Music of Israel . . . Through 5000 Years. Norton. $5

Hicks, Ami M. Everyday Art. Dutton. $3

Lewisohn, Sam A. Painters and Personality. Harper. $5

Marek, George R. Front Seat at the Opera. Crown. $4

Moore, Douglas. From Madrigal to Modern Music. Norton. $4.50

* Oglesby, Catharine. Modern Primitive Arts of Mexico, Guatemala and the Southwest. McGraw. $3

Robinson, Ethel F., and Robinson, Thomas P. Houses in America. Viking. $4

Schneider, Elisabeth. Aesthetic Motive. Macmillan. $2.50

Wilson, Carol G. Gump's Treasure Trade. Crowell. $5

Wright, Frank L. When Democracy Builds. Univ. of Chicago Press. $5

Wyler, Seymour. Book of Old Silver. Crown. $4

MODERN GUIDEPOSTS

† Banning, Margaret C. Letters to Susan. Harper. $1.50

* Boone, John A. You Are the Adventure. Prentice-Hall. $2.75

Brynes, Asher. Revolution Comes of Age. Rinehart. $2.50

* Butler, Nicholas M. Philosophy. Columbia Univ. Press. $1.25

Cousins, Norman. Modern Man Is Obsolete. Viking. $1

Edman, Irwin. Candle in the Dark. Viking. $1.25

Ellenwood, James L. It Runs in the Family. Scribner. $2.50

————— There's No Place Like Home. Scribner. $2.50

Feather, William. The Business of Life. Simon. $3.50

* Garrett, Eileen J. Awareness. Creative Age. $2.50

Giles, Ray. How to Retire—and Enjoy It. McGraw. $3

Goode, Kenneth M. How to Win What You Want. Prentice-Hall. $2.50

Hutchinson, Eliot D. How to Think Creatively. Abingdon-Cokesbury. $2.75

Ingram, Karl C. Winning Your Way with People. McGraw. $3

Jones, Ernest. What Is Psychoanalysis? International Universities Press. $2

Lamont, Corliss. Humanism as a Philosophy. Philosophical Library. $3.79

Liebman, Joshua L. Peace of Mind. Simon. $2.50

Lurton, Douglas. Make the Most of Your Life. McGraw. $2.50

Mangan, James T. Knack of Selling Yourself. Grosset. $1.49

Maritain, Jacques. The Person and the Common Good. Scribner. $2

Oliver, John R. Fear. Macmillan. $2.75

Osborn, Alexander F. Your Creative Power. How to Use Imagination. Scribner. $3

Panzer, Martin. Get a Kick out of Living. McGraw. $2.25

——— It's Your Future. McGraw. $2.75

* Peale, Norman V. A Guide to Confident Living. Prentice-Hall. $2.75

Preston, George H. Substance of Mental Health. Rinehart. $2

* Robinson, James H. Mind in the Making. Harper. $1.50

Santayana, George. Dialogues in Limbo. Scribner. $3

* Sartre, Jean-Paul. Existentialism. Philosophical Library. $2.75

Somerville, John. The Philosophy of Peace. Gaer. $3

* Strecker, Edward A., and others. Discovering Ourselves. Macmillan. $3.50

* Titus, Pauline W. How to Conquer Shyness. Funk. $2.85

Trine, Ralph W. Power That Wins. Bobbs. $2

Wahl, Jean A. Short History of Existentialism. Philosophical Library. $2.75

White, Stewart E. With Folded Wings. Dutton. $2.75

† Wilson, Margery. Charm. Stokes. $2.75

Woolf, James D., and Roth, Charles B. How to Use Your Imagination to Make Money. McGraw. $2.95

LITERARY BACKGROUNDS

Bespaloff, Rachel. On the Iliad. Pantheon Books. $2.50

Cather, Willa S. On Writing. Knopf. $2.25

Davis, Herbert. Satire of Jonathan Swift. Macmillan. $2

Dunn, Esther. Shakespeare in America. Macmillan. $3.50

Gide, André. Shakespeare's Hamlet. (Bi-lingual) Pantheon Books.
$2

Sartre, Jean-Paul. What Is Literature? Philosophical Library. $4.50

Spell, Jefferson. Contemporary Spanish-American Fiction. Univ. of
North Carolina Press. $3.50

Sper, Felix. From Native Roots, A Panorama of Our Regional
Drama. Caxton. $4

Tate, Allen. On the Limits of Poetry. Morrow. $4

* Wolfe, Thomas. The Story of a Novel. Scribner. $2

WILDERNESS LORE

Barbour, Thomas. A Naturalist's Scrapbook. Harvard Univ. Press.
$3

Bauer, Margaret J. Animal Babies. Donohue. $2

Beebe, Charles William. Book of Bays. Harcourt. $3.50

———— High Jungle. Duell. $4.50

† Behan, John M. Dogs of War. Scribner. $3.50

† Buck, Frank. On Jungle Trails. Lippincott. $2.50

Carhart, Arthur. Hi, Stranger: The Complete Guide to Dude
Ranches. Ziff-Davis. $3

Chapman, Wendell, and Chapman, Lucie. Wilderness Wanderers.
Scribner. $3.75

Devoe, Alan. Speaking of Animals. Creative Age. $3

† Ditmars, Raymond L. Snakes of the World. Macmillan. $2.95

Hornaday, William T. Tales from Nature's Wonderland. Scribner. $2.75

Jefferies, Richard. Old House at Coate. Harvard Univ. Press. $3.75

McKenny, Margaret, and Johnston, Edith F. Book of Wild Flowers.
Macmillan. $2.50

Mills, Enos A. The Grizzly. Houghton. $3

Peattie, Donald C. Flowering Earth. Putnam. $3

*† Pinkerton, Kathrene. Bright with Silver: Story of the Silver Fox. Sloane. $3.75

Rush, William M. Wild Animals of the Rockies. Harper. $3

Sutton, George M. Birds in the Wilderness. Macmillan. $4

Teale, Edwin W. Days Without Time. Dodd. $6

———— Lost Woods: Adventures of a Naturalist. Dodd. $5

Vernon, Arthur. History and Romance of the Horse. Dover. $3.75

*† Verrill, Alpheus H. Young Collector's Handbook. McBride. $2.75

Wheeler, Ruth. We Follow the Western Trail. Macmillan. $2

*† Young, Thomas. Dogs for Democracy. Beechhurst. $1

FAITH FOR ALL

Akhilananda, Swami. Hindu View of Christ. Philosophical Library. $3

Augustine, Saint. Faith, Hope and Charity. Newman Bookshop. $2.50

Bach, Marcus L. Report to Protestants. Bobbs. $3

Bainton, Roland H., ed. and tr. The Martin Luther Christmas Book. Westminster. $2.50

Bartlett, Gene E. The News in Religion and Other Sermons. Abingdon-Cokesbury. $1.75

Barton, Bruce. What Can a Man Believe? Grosset. 75c

Berger, Elmer. Jewish Dilemma. Devin-Adair. $3

Bible. Bible Designed to Be Read as Living Literature. Simon. $3.95

———— Book of Ruth. Heritage. $5

———— Holy Bible. American Revision Committee: Standard Edition. Nelson. $5.50

———— One Story; the Life of Christ, by Manuel Komroff. Dutton. $2.75

Bishop, Claire H. France Alive. McMullen. $3

Briggs, Everett F. New Dawn in Japan. Longmans. $2.75

Browne, Lewis. Stranger Than Fiction: A Short History of the Jews. Macmillan. $2

Browne, Lewis. World's Great Scriptures. Macmillan. $5

Clough, William A. Father We Thank Thee: Graces and Prayers for the Home. Abingdon-Cokesbury. $1.25

Cowles, Edward S. Don't Be Afraid! Wilcox & Follett. $2.50

Falvey, Hal. Ten Seconds That Will Change Your Life. Wilcox & Follett. $1

Farmer, Herbert H. God and Men. Abingdon-Cokesbury. $2

Finegan, Jack. Light from the Ancient Past. Princeton Univ. Press. $6

Fox, Emmet. Sermon on the Mount. Harper. $1

Frank, Waldo. The Jew in Our Day. Duell. $2.50

Freud, Sigmund. The Future of an Illusion. Liveright. $2.50

Gaer, Joseph. How the Great Religions Began. Dodd. $3

George, Father, pseud. God's Underground. Appleton. $3

Goldberg, Israel. Israel: A History of the Jewish People. World Pub. $4

Goodspeed, Edgar J. How to Read the Bible. Winston. $2

———— Paul, a Biography. Winston. $2.50

———— Story of the Apocrypha. Univ. of Chicago Press. $2.50

Grierson, Herbert, ed. And the Third Day . . . , a Record of Hope and Fulfilment. Macmillan. $3.50

Hoh, Paul J., and Hoh, Philip R. Two Minutes with God: A Book of Devotions for Homes with Children. Abingdon-Cokesbury. $1.50

Howard, Peter. Ideas Have Legs. Coward. $2.50

Johnson, George, Msgr., and Slavin, Robert J. Better Men for Better Times. Catholic Univ. Press. $1.50

Johnstone, Verney. The Story of the Prayer Book in England and America. Morehouse-Gorham. $2

Kleiser, Grenville. Taking God into Partnership. Funk. $1.50

*† Knox, Ronald. The Creed in Slow Motion. Sheed. $2.50

† ———— The Mass in Slow Motion. Sheed. $2.50

Landman, Solomon, and Efron, Benjamin. Story Without End: An Informal History of the Jewish People. Holt. $3

Latourette, Kenneth S. The Christian Outlook. Harper. $2.50

Learsi, Rufus. Israel: A History of the Jewish People. World Pub. $5

Lewis, Clive S. Great Divorce. Macmillan. $1.50

Liebman, Joshua L., ed. Psychiatry and Religion. Beacon Press. $2

Link, Henry C. Rediscovery of Morals. Dutton. $2.50

Man's Destiny in Eternity. Beacon Press. $2.75

† Manwell, Reginald D., and Fahs, Sophia L. Church across the Street. Beacon Press. $2

Morgan, George C. Music of Life. Revell. $1

Morgan, Thomas B. Speaking of Cardinals. Putnam. $3

Oxnam, Garfield B. Behold Thy Mother. Macmillan. $1.25

Park, William E. The Quest for Inner Peace. Macmillan. $2.50

Parsons, Wilfred. The First Freedom: Considerations on Church and State in the U. S. McMullen. $2.25

Peale, Norman V. Guideposts: Personal Messages of Inspiration and Faith. Prentice-Hall. $1.95

Rhoades, Winfred. Great Adventure of Living. Lippincott. $2

Rice, Merton S. My Father's World. Abingdon-Cokesbury. $1.75

Rowley, Harold H. The Re-discovery of the Old Testament. Westminster. $3.50

Runbeck, Margaret L. Answer Without Ceasing. Houghton. $3

Samuel, Maurice. Prince of the Ghetto. Jewish Pub. Society

Sargent, Daniel. Our Land and Our Lady. Longmans. $3

Schroeder, John C. Modern Man and the Cross. Scribner. $1.50

Scott, John F. The Religion of the Lord's Prayer. Abingdon-Cokesbury. $1

Smart, Wyatt A. Spiritual Gospel. Abingdon-Cokesbury. $1

Sneed, James R. How to Live Effectively. Revell. $1.50

* Stroup, Herbert H. A Symphony of Prayer. Judson. $3.50

Suter, John W., and Cleaveland, George J. American Book of Common Prayer, Its Origin and Development. Oxford Univ. Press. $1.50

Thomas à Kempis. Imitation of Christ, ed. by Klein. Harper. $3.50
Underhill, Evelyn. Collected Papers of . . . . Longmans. $1.75
Van Paassen, Pierre. Why Jesus Died. Dial. $3
Visser't Hooft, Willem A. Kingship of Christ. Harper. $1.75

FAVORITE ESSAYS AND LEGENDS

Barbeau, Charles M., and Melvin, Grace. The Indian Speaks. Caxton. $3

Borland, Harold G. American Year. Simon. $3.50

Campbell, Camilla, and McKinney, Ena. Star Mountain and Other Legends of Mexico. McGraw. $2.50

Cather, Willa S. Not under Forty. Knopf. $2

Davis, Edwin A. Of the Night Wind's Telling: Legends from the Valley of Mexico. Univ. of Oklahoma Press. $3

Gard, Robert E. Wisconsin Is My Doorstep. Longmans. $3.50

Gibran, Kahlil. Nymphs of the Valley. Knopf. $2.50

Greene, Ward, ed. Star Reporters and 34 of Their Stories. Random. $3

Heine, Heinrich. Germany, a Winter's Tale, 1844. Fischer. $2.75

Hubbard, Elbert. A Message to Garcia and Other Essays. Crowell. 65c

Humphrey, Zephine. Beloved Community. Dutton. $1.88

Inge, William R. Our Present Discontents. Putnam. $3.50

A Lady's Pleasure, the Modern Woman's Treasury of Good Reading. Penn Pub. Corp. $2.75

* McCormick, Dell J. Tall Timber Tales. Caxton. $2.60

Maugham, Somerset. Writer's Notebook. Doubleday. $4

Parsons, Alice. The Mountain. Dutton. $2.50

Priestley, John. Delight. Harper. $2.50

Ramuz, Charles. What Is Man? Pantheon Books. $2.75

Russian Fairy Tales. Pantheon Books. $7.50

Scandalous Adventures of Reynard the Fox, a Modern Version. Knopf. $3

† Stevens, James. Paul Bunyan. Knopf. $3

Thoreau, Henry. Walden. Dodd, Mead. $5

Treasury of the World's Great Letters. Simon. $3.95

*† Untermeyer, Louis. The Wonderful Adventures of Paul Bunyan. Heritage. $3

Warner, Frances. Surprising the Family. Houghton. $1.50

POTPOURRI

Barnes, Duane C. Wordlore. Dutton. $2.25

Copeland, Lewis. Toasts for All Occasions. Halcyon House. $1.50

Duff, Annis. Bequest of Wings: A Family's Pleasure with Books. Viking. $2.50

Feibleman, James. Theory of Human Culture. Duell. $5

Gardiner, Harold C. The Great Books; A Christian Appraisal. Devin-Adair Co. $2

† Hickok, Eliza M. The Quiz Kids. Houghton. $2.50

Hush, Howard. Eastwick, U. S. A. Dutton. $3

Huxley, Aldous. Ends and Means, an Inquiry into the Nature of Ideals. Harper. $3

Lee, Joshua B. How to Hold an Audience Without a Rope. Ziff-Davis. $3

Miers, Earl. Bookmaking and Kindred Amenities. Rutgers Univ. Press. $3.50

New Comprehensive Standard Dictionary. (Definitions in 12-point, words in larger type.) Funk. $3

† Pierce, Wellington G. Youth Comes of Age. McGraw. $3.50

Rogers, Frances, and Beard, Alice. 5000 Years of Glass. Lippincott. $3.75

Schauffler, Robert. The Days We Celebrate. Dodd, Mead. 4v. $2.50 ea.

Van Doren, Mark. Liberal Education. Holt. $3

Wilkins, Harold. Marvels of Modern Mechanics. Dutton. $3

Winterich, John T. Primer of Book-collecting. Greenberg. $3

59

Juvenile Books

** Armer, Laura Adams. Forest Pool. Longmans. $2.50

Atwater, Richard T., and Atwater, Florence H. Mr. Popper's Penguins. Little. $2.50

Baker, Charlotte. Necessary Nellie. Coward. $2.50

———— Nellie and the Mayor's Hat. Coward. $2.50

Baker, Elizabeth W. Sonny-Boy Sim. Rand. $1

** Bannon, Laura. Gregorio and the White Llama. Whitman. $2

Beaty, John Y. Baby Whale, Sharp Ears. Lippincott. $2

Bishop, Claire Huchet. Pancakes-Paris. Viking. $2

Blough, Glenn O. Monkey with a Notion. Holt. $2.25

Bontemps, Arna, and Conroy, Jack. Fast Sooner Hound. Houghton. $2

** Brock, Emma L. Here Comes Kristie. Knopf. $2

** ———— Kristie and the Colt and the Others. Knopf. $2

** ———— Topsy-turvy Family. Knopf. $2

Bronson, Wilfrid S. Pinto's Journey. Messner. $2.50

Brown, Marcia. Henry-Fisherman. Scribner. $2

Buff, Mary, and Buff, Conrad. Peter's Pinto. Viking. $2

Clark, Margery. Poppy Seed Cakes. Doubleday. $2.50

DeAngeli, Marguerite. Henner's Lydia. Doubleday. $2.50

———— Yonie Wondernose. Doubleday. $2

DeLeeuw, Adèle. Nobody's Doll. Little. $2

Estes, Eleanor. Hundred Dresses. Harcourt. $2.50

Faulkner, Georgene. Melindy's Happy Summer. Messner. $2.50

Flack, Marjorie, and Larsson, Karl. Pedro. Macmillan. $2.50

Foster, Elizabeth. House at Noddy Cove. Houghton. $2.25

** Gall, Alice, and Crew, Fleming. Ringtail. Oxford Univ. Press. $1.50

Gannett, Ruth Stiles. My Father's Dragon. Random. $2

Grey, Eve. Elsa's Secret. Doubleday. $2.25

** Haywood, Carolyn. "B" Is for Betsy. Harcourt. $2.25
** —————— Back to School with Betsy. Harcourt. $2.50
** —————— Betsy and Billy. Harcourt. $2.25
** —————— Betsy and the Boys. Harcourt. $2
** —————— Eddie and the Fire Engine. Morrow. $2
** —————— Here's a Penny. Harcourt. $2.50
** —————— Little Eddie. Morrow. $2.50
** —————— Penny and Peter. Harcourt. $2.25
** —————— Penny Goes to Camp. Morrow. $2
** —————— Two and Two Are Four. Harcourt. $2.50
  Hunt, Mabel Leigh. Benjie's Hat. Lippincott. $2.25
** Hutchinson, Veronica S., comp. Fireside Stories. Putnam. $3
** Johnson, Margaret S. Snowshoe Paws. Morrow. $2
** Johnson, Margaret S., and Johnson, Helen L. Barney of the North.
        Harcourt. $2.25
** —————— Dixie Dobie. Harcourt. $2
** —————— Rolf, an Elkhound of Norway. Harcourt. $2.25
** —————— Smallest Puppy. Harcourt. $1.75
  Johnson, Siddie Joe. Debby. Longmans. $2.25
  Jones, Elizabeth Orton. Big Susan. Macmillan. $2
  Kinney, Harrison. Lonesome Bear. McGraw. $2
  Lane, Carl D. River Dragon. Little. $2.50
** Lattimore, Eleanor F. Bayou Boy. Morrow. $2
** —————— Davy of the Everglades. Morrow. $2
** —————— Deborah's White Winter. Morrow. $2
** —————— Peachblossom. Harcourt. $2
** —————— Three Little Chinese Girls. Morrow. $2
** LeSueur, Meridel. Little Brother of the Wilderness. Knopf. $2.50
** —————— Nancy Hanks of Wilderness Road. Knopf. $2.50
  Lovelace, Maud Hart. Betsy-Tacy. Crowell. $2
  —————— Betsy-Tacy and Tib. Crowell. $2
  —————— Over the Big Hill. Crowell. $2
  Lownsbery, Eloise. Marta the Doll. Longmans. $2
** Mason, Miriam E. Happy Jack. Macmillan. $1.50

** Mason, Miriam E. Little Jonathan. Macmillan. $1.50
** ———— Middle Sister. Macmillan. $1.75
** ———— Pony Called Lightning. Macmillan. $1.75
** ———— Susannah, the Pioneer Cow. Macmillan. $1.50
   Meadowcroft, Enid L. On Indian Trails with Daniel Boone. Crowell.
      $2.50
** Milhous, Katherine. Lovina: A Story of the Pennsylvania Country.
      Scribner. $1.50
** Reely, Mary Katharine. Seatmates. Watts. $2
** Rostron, Richard. Sorcerer's Apprentice. Morrow. $2.50
   Schram, Constance Wiel. Olaf, Lofoten Fisherman. Longmans.
      $1.75
** Stilwell, Alison. Chin Ling: The Chinese Cricket. Macmillan. $2.25
   Stong, Phil. Honk: The Moose. Dodd. $2.75
** Tousey, Sanford. Cowboy Tommy. Doubleday. $1.50
** Tregarthen, Enys. Doll Who Came Alive. Day. $2.25
** Walsh, Mary. Mullingar Heifer. Knopf. $1.75
** ———— Widow Woman and Her Goat. Knopf. $1.75
** Woolley, Catherine. David's Railroad. Morrow. $2
** ———— Two Hundred Pennies. Morrow. $2

STORIES FOR CHILDREN NINE TO TWELVE

   Alcott, Louisa May. Jo's Boys. Grosset. $1.25
   ———— Little Women. World Pub. $1
   Angelo, Valenti. Hill of Little Miracles. Viking. $2.50
   Bailey, Carolyn Sherwin. Miss Hickory. Viking. $2.50
   Banning, Nina Lloyd. Pit Pony. Knopf. $2
   Barnes, Nancy. Wonderful Year. Messner. $2.50
   Bothwell, Jean. Little Flute Player. Morrow. $2
   ———— River Boy of Kashmir. Morrow. $2
** ———— Thirteenth Stone. Harcourt. $2
   Bowers, Gwendolyn. Adventures of Philippe: A Story of Old
      Kebec. Aladdin. $2.50

Brink, Carol Ryrie. All over Town. Macmillan. $2.50
—————— Anything Can Happen on the River. Macmillan. $2.50
—————— Caddie Woodlawn. Macmillan. $2.50
—————— Magical Melons. Macmillan. $2.50
Brock, Emma L. Heedless Susan. Knopf. $2
Brooks, Walter R. Freddy Goes to Florida. Knopf. $2.50
** Buck, Pearl S. Big Wave. Day. $2
Campbell, Camilla. Bartletts of Box B Ranch. McGraw. $2.25
Carroll, Lewis. Alice in Wonderland and Through the Looking Glass. Grosset. $1.25
Ceder, Georgiana D. Ethan, the Shepherd Boy. Abingdon-Cokesbury. $2
Clymer, Eleanor. Trolley Car Family. McKay. $2
Collodi, Carlo. Pinocchio. Lippincott. $2.50
** Dalgliesh, Alice. Davenports and Cherry Pie. Scribner. $2.50
Daringer, Helen F. Pilgrim Kate. Harcourt. $2.50
DeAngeli, Marguerite. Door in the Wall. Doubleday. $2.50
—————— Elin's Amerika. Doubleday. $2.50
—————— Up the Hill. Doubleday. $2
Douglas, Emily Taft. Appleseed Farm. Abingdon-Cokesbury. $1.50
Dusoe, Robert C. Three Without Fear. Longmans. $2.25
Eames, Genevieve Torrey. Horse to Remember. Messner. $2.50
Edmonds, Walter D. Matchlock Gun. Dodd. $2.50
Enright, Elizabeth. Melendy Family. Rinehart. $2.95
Evernden, Margery. Runaway Apprentice. Random. $2.50
Eyre, Katherine W. Spurs for Antonia. Oxford Univ. Press. $2
Fenton, Edward. Us and the Duchess. Doubleday. $2
Franklin, George C. Tricky: The Adventures of a Red Fox. Houghton. $2.25
Friedman, Frieda. Sundae with Judy. Morrow. $2.50
Fuller, Alice C. Gold for the Grahams. Messner. $2.50
Garst, Shannon. Cowboy Boots. Abingdon-Cokesbury. $2
Gates, Doris. Sarah's Idea. Viking. $1.50
Gibson, Katharine. Arrow Fly Home. Longmans. $2

Godden, Rumer. Dolls' House. Viking. $2.50

** Goetz, Delia. Burro of Barnegat Road. Harcourt. $2

** Henderson, LeGrand. Augustus and the Mountains. Bobbs. $2.50

** —————— Augustus Goes South. Bobbs. $2.50

Henry, Marguerite. Benjamin West and His Cat Grimalkin. Bobbs. $2.50

—————— Misty of Chincoteague. Rand. $2.75

—————— Sea Star, Orphan of Chincoteague. Rand. $2.75

Holberg, Ruth Langland. At the Sign of the Golden Anchor. Doubleday. $2.25

—————— Rowena Carey. Doubleday. $2.50

—————— Wonderful Voyage. Doubleday. $2

Holberg, Ruth L., and Holberg, Richard A. Oh Susannah. Doubleday. $2

Johnson, Siddie Joe. Susan's Year. Longmans. $2.25

Jones, Elizabeth Orton. Twig. Macmillan. $2

Karolyi, Erna M. Summer to Remember. McGraw. $2

** Kipling, Rudyard. Just So Stories. Doubleday. $2.50

** Lang, Don. On the Dark of the Moon. Oxford Univ. Press. $2

Lenski, Lois. Cotton in My Sack. Lippincott. $2.50

—————— Judy's Journey. Lippincott. $2.50

—————— Strawberry Girl. Lippincott. $2.50

Lofting, Hugh. Story of Dr. Dolittle. Lippincott. $2.75

Lovelace, Maud Hart. Down Town. Crowell. $2

McMeekin, Isabel M. Journey Cake. Messner. $2.50

—————— Juba's New Moon. Messner. $2.50

—————— Kentucky Derby Winner. McKay. $2.50

McSwigan, Marie. Snow Treasure. Dutton. $2.50

Marshall, Dean. Invisible Island. Dutton. $2.50

—————— Long White Month. Dutton. $2.50

Martin, Dahris. Adventure in Ireland. Messner. $2.50

Meader, Stephen W. Skippy's Family. Harcourt. $2.25

Morrow, Honoré. On to Oregon! Morrow. $2.50

O'Faolain, Eileen. Miss Pennyfeather and the Pooka. Random. $2

Otis, James. Toby Tyler, or Ten Weeks with a Circus. World Pub. $1.25
Pyle, Howard. Pepper and Salt. Harper. $1.50
Ruskin, John. King of the Golden River. World Pub. $1.25
Sauer, Julia L. Fog Magic. Viking. $2
** Sewell, Anna. Black Beauty. Grosset. $2
Sidney, Margaret. Five Little Peppers and How They Grew. Grosset. $2
Smith, Eunice Young. Jennifer Wish. Bobbs. $2.50
Spyri, Johanna. Heidi. Grosset. $2
Stone, Eugenia. Secret of the Bog. Holiday House. $2.25
Treffinger, Carolyn. Li Lun, Lad of Courage. Abingdon-Cokesbury. $2.50
** Tregarthen, Enys. White Ring. Harcourt. $2
Turnbull, Agnes S. Elijah the Fishbite. Macmillan. $2.50
Van Stockum, Hilda. Andries. Viking. $2.50
** ———— Gerrit and the Organ. Viking. $2.50
———— Pegeen. Viking. $2.50
** Von Hagen, Christine. Forgotten Finca. Nelson. $2.50
Warren, Billy. Ride, Cowboy, Ride. McKay. $2.50
Wilder, Laura Ingalls. By the Shores of Silver Lake. Harper. $2
———— Farmer Boy. Harper. $2
** ———— Little House in the Big Woods. Harper. $2
———— On the Banks of Plum Creek. Harper. $2
Wilson, Hazel. Island Summer. Abingdon-Cokesbury. $2
Yates, Elizabeth. Mountain Born. Coward. $2.50

STORIES FOR JUNIOR TEENS

Allen, Merritt Parmelee. Battle Lanterns. Longmans. $2.50
———— Red Heritage. Longmans. $2.25
Baker, Elizabeth W. Stocky, Boy of West Texas. Winston. $2
Bell, Margaret E. Watch for a Tall White Sail. Morrow. $2.50
Bird, Dorothy M. Granite Harbor. Macmillan. $2

Brill, Ethel C. Copper Country Adventure. McGraw. $2.50

———— Madeleine Takes Command. McGraw. $2

Caudill, Rebecca. Barrie and Daughter. Viking. $2

Cavanna, Betty. Going on Sixteen. Westminster. $2

Clemens, Samuel L. Adventures of Tom Sawyer. Grosset. $1.25

Cooper, James Fenimore. Deerslayer. Scribner. $2.50

———— Last of the Mohicans. Scribner. $2.50

Davis, Robert. Partners of Powder Hole. Holiday House. $2.25

Defoe, Daniel. Robinson Crusoe. Grosset. $1.25

Dickson, Marguerite. Bramble Bush. Nelson. $2

———— Turn in the Road. Nelson. $2.50

duBois, William Pène. Twenty-one Balloons. Viking. $2.50

Du Soe, Robert C. Sea Boots. Longmans. $2.50

Edmonds, Walter D. Tom Whipple. Dodd. $2.50

Emery, Anne. Senior Year. Westminster. $2.50

Farley, Walter. Island Stallion. Random. $2

Fenner, Phyllis R. Horses, Horses, Horses. Watts. $2.50

George, John L., and George, Jean. Vulpes the Red Fox. Dutton. $2.50

Gray, Elizabeth Janet. Adam of the Road. Viking. $2.75

Hayes, Marjorie. Green Peace. Lippincott. $2

Henry, Marguerite. King of the Wind. Rand. $2.75

Irving, Washington. Bold Dragoon and Other Ghostly Tales. Knopf. $2.75

James, Will. Smoky. Scribner. $2.50

Kjelgaard, Jim. Big Red. Holiday House. $2.50

———— Kalak of the Ice. Holiday House. $2.50

———— Nose for Trouble. Holiday House. $2.50

———— Snow Dog. Holiday House. $2.50

Lewis, Elizabeth Foreman. Young Fu of the Upper Yangtze. Winston. $2.50

Lovelace, Maud Hart. Carney's House Party. Crowell. $2.50

———— Heaven to Betsy. Crowell. $2.50

Low, Elizabeth. High Harvest. Harcourt. $2.50

Meader, Stephen W. Boy with a Pack. Harcourt. $2.50
——— Cedar's Boy. Harcourt. $2.50
——— Jonathan Goes West. Harcourt. $2.25
——— Red Horse Hill. Harcourt. $2.50
——— River of Wolves. Harcourt. $2.50
Meadowcroft, Enid L. By Secret Railway. Crowell. $3
Means, Florence Crannell. Assorted Sisters. Houghton. $2.75
——— Great Day in the Morning. Houghton. $2.75
Nolan, Jeannette C. Treason at the Point. Messner. $2.50
Patterson, Emma L. Midnight Patriot. Longmans. $2.75
Pinkerton, Kathrene. Good Partner. Harcourt. $2.50
——— Silver Strain. Harcourt. $2
——— Windigo. Harcourt. $2.50
Reinherz, Nathan. Trumpets at the Crossroads. Crowell. $2.75
Seredy, Kate. Good Master. Viking. $2.50
——— Singing Tree. Viking. $2.50
——— White Stag. Viking. $2.50
Shapiro. Irwin. Joe Magarac and His U. S. A. Citizen Papers. Messner. $2.50
Simon, Charlie May. Joe Mason: Apprentice to Audubon. Dutton. $2.50
** Singh, Reginald L., and Lownsbery, Eloise. Gift of the Forest. Longmans. $2.50
Snedeker, Caroline Dale. Downright Dency. Doubleday. $2.25
Sperry, Armstrong. Call It Courage. Macmillan. $2.50
——— Rain Forest. Macmillan. $2.50
Tunis, John R. All-American. Harcourt. $2.50
——— Highpockets. Morrow. $2.50
——— Keystone Kids. Harcourt. $2
——— Rookie of the Year. Harcourt. $2.75
Waldeck, Theodore J. Jamba the Elephant. Viking. $2
——— White Panther. Viking. $2
Wilder, Laura Ingalls. Little House on the Prairie. Harper. $2
——— Little Town on the Prairie. Harper. $2

Wilder, Laura Ingalls. Long Winter. Harper. $2
——— These Happy Golden Years. Harper. $2

FAIRY TALES—FOLKLORE—LEGENDS

Andersen, Hans Christian. Andersen's Fairy Tales. Coward. $2.50.
4-6
——— Emperor's New Clothes. Houghton. $2. 3-5
** Belpré, Pura. Perez and Martina. Warne. $2. 2-4
Boggs, Ralph S., and Davis, Mary Gould. Three Golden Oranges.
Longmans. $2.50. 4-6
Chase, Richard, ed. Grandfather Tales. Houghton. $2.75. 4-7
Fahs, Sophia L. From Long Ago and Many Lands. Beacon Press.
$2.50. 3-5
Fenner, Phyllis R., comp. Adventure: Rare and Magical. Knopf.
$2.50. 5-8
——— Fools and Funny Fellows. Knopf. $2.50. 4-7
——— Giants and Witches and a Dragon or Two. Knopf. $2.50.
4-6
——— There Was a Horse: Folk Tales from Many Lands. Knopf.
$2.50. 6-8
Grimm, Jakob L. K., and Grimm, Wilhelm K. Grimm's Fairy Tales.
Grosset. $3. 4-6
——— House in the Wood, and Other Fairy Stories. Warne. $2.25.
3-5
——— Tales from Grimm. Coward. $2.75. 4-6
——— Three Gay Tales from Grimm. Coward. $1.50. 3-5
Harris, Joel C. Favorite Uncle Remus. Houghton. $3. 5-8
Hatch, Mary C. More Danish Tales. Harcourt. $2.50. 3-5
——— 13 Danish Tales. Harcourt. $2.50. 4-8
** Hutchinson, Veronica, comp. Chimney Corner Fairy Tales. Min-
ton, Balch. $3. 3-5
Jacobs, Joseph, ed. English Fairy Tales. Putnam. $2. 4-6
——— More English Fairy Tales. Putnam. $2. 4-6

** Kelsey, Alice G. Once the Hodja. Longmans. $2.25. 4-6

** McCormick, Dell J. Paul Bunyan Swings His Axe. Caxton. $2.60. 4-6

MacManus, Seumas. Well o' the World's End: Irish Folk Tales. Devin-Adair. $2.50. 4-6

McSpadden, Joseph Walker. Robin Hood and His Merry Outlaws. World Pub. $1.25. 6-8

Sawyer, Ruth. Picture Tales from Spain. Lippincott. $1.75. 4-6

Uchida, Yoshiko. Dancing Kettle and Other Japanese Folk Tales. Harcourt. $2.25. 3-5

Undset, Sigrid. True and Untrue and Other Norse Tales. Knopf. $2.50. 4-7

** Watkins, Hope Brister. Cunning Fox and Other Tales. Knopf. $2. 3-5

POETRY

Adshead, Gladys L., and Duff, Annis, comps. Inheritance of Poetry. Houghton. $3.50. 8-9

McFarland, Wilma, ed. For a Child: Great Poems Old and New. Westminster. $2.50. 2-5

Millay, Edna St. V. Edna St. Vincent Millay's Poems Selected for Young People. Harper. $2.50. 6-9

Sandburg, Carl. Early Moon. Harcourt. $3. 5-9

Stevenson, Robert Louis. Child's Garden of Verses. Oxford Univ. Press. $2.50. 1-4

Thompson, Blanche Jennings, ed. Silver Pennies. Macmillan. $1.25. 3-8

Untermeyer, Louis, ed. Rainbow in the Sky. Harcourt. $3.75. 3-8

CHRISTMAS AND OTHER HOLIDAYS

Association for Childhood Education. Told under the Christmas Tree. Macmillan. $3. 4-7

** Bianco, Pamela. Joy and the Christmas Angel. Oxford Univ. Press.
    $1.75. 3-5

Dickens, Charles. Christmas Carol. Macmillan. $1.50. 7-9

Fenner, Phyllis. Feast and Frolics: Special Stories for Special Days.
    Knopf. $2.50. 4-7

Harper, Wilhelmina. Easter Chimes. Dutton. $2. 4-6

Lathrop, Dorothy P. Angel in the Woods. Macmillan. $2. 1-3

** Sawyer, Ruth. Christmas Anna Angel. Viking. $2. 3-5

———— Long Christmas. Viking. $2.50. 4-9

———— This Is the Christmas: A Serbian Folk Tale. Horn Book.
    $1. 5-6

Sechrist, Elizabeth H. Heigh-ho for Hallowe'en. Macrae. $2.50. 4-8

———— Red Letter Days: A Book of Holiday Customs. Macrae.
    $2.50. 5-7

Smith, Irene. Santa Claus Book. Watts. $2.50. 3-5

Vance, Marguerite. While Shepherds Watched. Dutton. $1. 2-4

BIOGRAPHY

** Aulaire, Ingri M.d', and Aulaire, Edgar P.d'. Abraham Lincoln.
    Doubleday. $2.50. 3-4

** ———— George Washington. Doubleday. $2.75. 3-5

———— Leif the Lucky. Doubleday. $2.50. 3-6

** Averill, Esther. Daniel Boone. Harper. $1.50. 3-6

Bakeless, John. Fighting Frontiersman: The Life of Daniel Boone.
    Morrow. $2.75. 7-9

Bryan, Florence Horn. Susan B. Anthony: Champion of Women's
    Rights. Messner. $2.75. 7-9

Daugherty, James. Daniel Boone. Viking. $3. 5-9

———— Poor Richard. Viking. $3. 7-9

** Deucher, Sybil. Edvard Grieg: Boy of the Northland. Dutton.
    $2.50. 4-7

Eaton, Jeanette. David Livingstone. Morrow. $3. 7-9

Eaton, Jeanette. Leader by Destiny: George Washington, Man and Patriot. Harcourt. $3.50. 7-9

———— Narcissa Whitman: Pioneer of Oregon. Harcourt. $2.50. 8-9

———— That Lively Man, Ben Franklin. Morrow. $2.50. 5-8

Ewen, David. Tales from the Vienna Woods: The Story of Johann Strauss. Holt. $3. 7-9

Fast, Howard. Haym Salomon: Son of Liberty. Messner. $2.75. 7-9

Foster, Genevieve. George Washington. Scribner. $2. 4-6

Garst, Shannon. Kit Carson: Trail Blazer and Scout. Messner. $2.75. 6-9

———— Sitting Bull: Champion of His People. Messner. $2.75. 6-9

Hodges, C. Walter. Columbus Sails. Coward. $3. 7-9

Holberg, Ruth Langland. Captain John Smith. Crowell. $2.50. 7-9

Holbrook, Stewart. America's Ethan Allen. Houghton. $2.50. 4-6

Humphreys, Dena. On Wings of Song: The Story of Mendelssohn. Holt. $3. 7-9

Jarden, Mary Louise. Young Brontës. Viking. $3. 7-9

Judson, Clara I. Soldier Doctor: The Story of Wm. Gorgas. Scribner. $2.50. 5-8

Kerr, Laura. Doctor Elizabeth. Nelson. $2.50. 7-9

Meigs, Cornelia. Invincible Louisa. Little. $2.50. 7-9

Newcomb, Covelle. Larger Than the Sky: A Story of James Cardinal Gibbons. Longmans. $2.75. 7-9

Nolan, Jeannette Covert. Florence Nightingale. Messner. $2.75. 6-9

Pace, Mildred Mastin. Clara Barton. Scribner. $2. 4-8

Purdy, Claire Lee. He Heard America Sing: The Story of Stephen Foster. Messner. $2.75. 6-8

Rourke, Constance. Audubon. Harcourt. $2.69. 7-9

———— Davy Crockett. Harcourt. $2.75. 7-9

Sandburg, Carl. Abe Lincoln Grows Up. Harcourt. $2.75. 7-9

Waugh, Elizabeth. Simón Bolívar: A Story of Courage. Macmillan. $3. 7-9

** Wheeler, Opal. Frederic Chopin, Son of Poland: Later Years. Dutton. $2.75. 4-6

** ———Handel at the Court of Kings. Dutton. $2.50. 4-6

** ——— Ludwig Beethoven and the Chiming Tower Bells. Dutton. $2.50. 4-7

** ——— Stephen Foster and His Little Dog Tray. Dutton. $2.50. 4-5

** Wheeler, Opal, and Deucher, Sybil. Edward MacDowell and His Cabin in the Pines. Dutton. $2.50. 4-6

** ——— Franz Schubert and His Merry Friends. Dutton. $2.50. 4-5

** ——— Joseph Haydn, the Merry Little Peasant. Dutton. $2.50. 4-5

** ——— Mozart, the Wonder Boy. Dutton. $2.50. 4-5

** ——— Sebastian Bach, the Boy from Thuringia. Dutton. $2.50. 5-8

RELIGION

Barnhart, Nancy. Lord Is My Shepherd. Scribner. $4.50. 3-6

Becker, May Lamberton. Rainbow Book of Bible Stories. World Pub. $1.25. 4-6

Fitch, Florence. One God: The Ways We Worship Him. Lothrop. $2.50. 5-9

——— Their Search for God: Ways of Worship in the Orient. Lothrop. $3. 6-9

Hartman, Gertrude. In Bible Days. Macmillan. $2.50. 6-9

** Petersham, Maud, and Petersham, Miska. Christ Child: As Told by Matthew and Luke. Doubleday. $2. 1-6

Raymond, Louise, ed. Child's Story of the Nativity. Random. $2. 2-5

NATURE—SCIENCE—MECHANICS

** Bridges, William. True Zoo Stories. Sloane. $2.50. 2-5

——— Wild Animals of the World. Garden City. $4.95. 5-9

** Brindze, Ruth. Gulf Stream. Vanguard. $2.50. 4-6

Britton, Katharine. What Makes It Tick? Houghton. $3. 5-8

** Bronson, Wilfrid S. Coyotes. Harcourt. $1.75. 2-5

** ———— Pollwiggle's Progress. Macmillan. $2.50. 3-5

** ———— Starlings. Harcourt. $2. 3-6

** ———— Turtles. Harcourt. $2. 3-6

** ———— Wonder World of Ants. Harcourt. $2. 4-6

Cothren, Marion B. This Is the Moon. Coward. $2. 6-9

Crouse, William Harry. Understanding Science. McGraw. $2.75. 6-9

Eberle, Irmengarde. Modern Medical Discoveries. Crowell. $2.50. 6-9

Gaul, Albro T. Picture Book of Insects. Lothrop. $1.50. 4-7

Hartman, Gertrude. Machines and the Men Who Made the World of Industry. Macmillan. $3.50. 6-9

Hogner, Dorothy Childs. Barnyard Family. Oxford Univ. Press. $2.75. 4-7

Huntington, Harriet E. Let's Go to the Seashore. Doubleday. $2.50. 2-5

Kane, Henry B. Tale of the Promethea Moth. Knopf. $1.75. 4-7

Lewellen, John. You and Atomic Energy. Childrens Press. $1.50. 6-8

** McClung, Robert M. Sphinx: The Story of a Caterpillar. Morrow. $2. 5-9

McMeekin, Isabel M. First Book of Horses. Watts. $1.50. 6-9

Mason, George F. Animal Homes. Morrow. $2. 5-8

———— Animal Sounds. Morrow. $2. 6-9

———— Animal Tracks. Morrow. $2. 4-7

———— Animal Weapons. Morrow. $2. 5-8

Smith, E. Boyd. So Long Ago. Houghton. $2. 3-5

Williamson, Margaret. First Book of Bugs. Watts. $1.50. 3-5

** Zim, Herbert S. Elephants. Morrow. $2. 2-4

** ———— Goldfish. Morrow. $2. 4-7

———— Homing Pigeons. Morrow. $2. 4-7

** ———— Rabbits. Morrow. $2. 4-7

** ———— Snakes. Morrow. $2. 3-6

SOCIAL SCIENCE—HISTORY—TRAVEL

Barnouw, Adriaan. Land of William of Orange. Lippincott. $2.25. 4-9

Bontemps, Arna. Story of the Negro. Knopf. $3. 7-9

** Cavanah, Frances. Our Country's Story. Rand. $2.50. 2-4

Dalgliesh, Alice. America Begins. Scribner. $2.75. 3-4

——— America Builds Homes. Scribner. $2.75. 3-4

** Daugherty, James. Wild Wild West. McKay. $2.50. 5-8

Elting, Mary. Trains at Work. Garden City. $1. 3-5

Evans, Eva Knox. All about Us. Capitol. $2. 4-8

Foster, Genevieve. Abraham Lincoln's World. Scribner. $3.50. 7-9

——— Augustus Caesar's World. Scribner. $3.50. 7-9

——— George Washington's World. Scribner. $3.50. 6-9

Galt, Tom. How the United Nations Works. Crowell. $2.50. 5-9

Gill, Richard C., and Hoke, Helen. Story of the Other America. Houghton. $3. 5-8

Goetz, Delia. Other Young Americans: Latin America's Young People. Morrow. $3.50. 7-9

** Goslin, Ryllis, and Goslin, Omar. Democracy. Harcourt. $2.50. 4-5

Hall-Quest, Olga W. How the Pilgrims Came to Plymouth. Dutton. $2.25. 4-6

——— Shrine of Liberty: The Alamo. Dutton. $2.25. 4-6

Hark, Ann. Story of the Pennsylvania Dutch. Harper. $1.50. 4-7

Hogarth, Grace Allen. Australia, the Island Continent. Houghton. $2. 5-8

Holling, Holling C. Book of Indians. Platt. $1.69. 4-6

** Leaf, Munro. Let's Do Better. Lippincott. $2. 3-6

Marriott, Alice. Indians on Horseback. Crowell. $3. 4-8

Olds, Elizabeth. Big Fire. Houghton. $2.50. 5-9

** ——— Riding the Rails. Houghton. $2.50. 2-4

** Petersham, Maud, and Petersham, Miska. American ABC. Macmillan. $2.50. 3-6

———— America's Stamps: Story of 100 Years of U. S. Postage Stamps. Macmillan. $3.50. 5-9

** Quinn, Vernon. Picture Map Geography of Mexico, Central America and the West Indies. Lippincott. $2.25. 4-7

** ———— Picture Map Geography of South America. Lippincott. $2.50. 4-6

** ———— Picture Map Geography of the Pacific Islands. Lippincott. $2.25. 5-8

** ———— Picture Map Geography of the U. S. Lippincott. $3. 4-6

Rothery, Agnes. Iceland Roundabout. Dodd. $2.75. 5-9

———— Scandinavian Roundabout. Dodd. $2.75. 6-9

** Shackelford, Jane Dabney. Child's Story of the Negro. Associated Pubs. $2.65. 3-5

Shippen, Katherine B. Great Heritage. Viking. $3.50. 7-9

Smither, Ethel L. Picture Book of Palestine. Abingdon-Cokesbury. $1. 3-6

Swift, Hildegarde Hoyt. North Star Shining: A Pictorial History of the American Negro. Morrow. $2.50. 7-9

This line is printed in 12 point type.

This is 14 point type.

This is 18 point type.

This is 24 point type.

This is 30 point.

This is 36 point.